SOULROT

SOUL ROT

And the Life and Times of THE PERFECT BLACK MAN

Book One of Three

* Series *
Escaping The Box

Interpreted By

Michael Mason Norman, ED.D.

Soul Rot Researcher,
Biographer, and Model Developer

Published by Michael Mason Norman, ED.D.
Minneapolis, 2011

Social-Political Fiction/Current Events
Commentaries/Education/Fictional Biography

The author is solely responsible for all commentaries,
stories, and observations. Any resemblances of characters,
places, events, etc., with real life individuals and places are
purely coincidental.

Michael Mason Norman, ED.D.
b. 1950

Soul Rot: And the Life and Times of the Perfect Black Man

ISBN-13: 978-1460946763
ISBN-10: 1460946766

First paperback edition

Contents

- Who are we without the Perfect Black Man and other perfect
- people?

- What does a Perfect Black Man cost society?

- Who is going to buy your wonderful lifestyles?

- Oh where oh where have all our myths gone? They ran far, so far away, said our souls.

Introduction

An interpreter's perspective on *why* the Perfect Black Man

exists. Note: the books do not require sequential reading of

chapters.

++

Soul Rot: Escaping The Box--is a series of three books
examining a set of attributes of a cohort of native-born African-
American men.   It is the first of several series on Soul Rot in
America.

Escaping The Box addresses a plight of an America, which
is regressing, if not retiring, from an ever-bright future. Indeed,
one perspective of the interpreter, depicts not only a "dumbing-
down" of America, but also a dulling of its collective senses. He
wonders if America is being systematically shocked and awed,
into socially destructive dementia? How? Through neglecting
and ignoring, time sensitive issues of historical and economic
relevance. Consequently, fulfilling an unstated preference by
certain parties, for supporting fact-adverse ideologies, which
worship unmistakable denials of unaccountable behaviors.

Consequently, when a country is quietly being sterilized
by fear and regressive tantrums; it entertains repressing the
future and promotes redesigned myths. From there it can hide
its eyes away from "unpleasant" things to remember. That is to
say, it must abandon progress. In so doing it sinks a selection of
the population into a quagmire of self-pity. Why? Because those
living in constant fear, believe a progressively oriented future
will not look as safe, as an envisioned past, Hidden in that past
we find where their emotional identities are protected.

Not surprisingly, they are at a minimum, unwilling to imagine others wanting to move the country forward into uncertainty. In particular, when they cannot imagine the possibilities of life, outside of having daily conversations with myths. Again imagine, listening to their dialogues, where they express how no one should progress beyond what is already known! It is a logic we will revisit later in another volume of the series. But let's continue...

A few personal thoughts

Consistent with my nature as a workaholic, I have spent years digesting reports, newspapers, websites, blogs, and magazine articles. I have met and watched the lives of thousands of people. My challenge has been to discern the plight of young Black men in our social development and support systems.

For instance, whether looking at publically or privately financed programs, it has become quite clear to me that these young men are facing systemically set odds against their collective futures. Yet, I started seeing some patterns in how their communities, families, and other support apparatus, where hedging against the future prospects of the young men.

The lives of these men are completed inside a box, with a specially designed roulette table set in its middle. On the table's board and wheel, you will notice that the number 6 is missing. The young men are represented as chips with only one value. The game's players are all factors, which influence a young, Perfect Black Man's future. The players have to remember only one rule: all odds favor the house (box.)

Let me make one very important point clear to all: I am not writing about young Black women. Because I do not feel qualified to write about their life situations. Obviously, you should expect to read indirect and direct references to women in the stories, etc.; as women are inevitably part of the lives of young men. But, I invite other writers to engage in completing that part of the picture. **Finally, others should also tackle the complete puzzle, and serve as the messengers of Hope and success for the future.**

Michael Mason Norman, ED.D.

THE PERFECT BLACK MAN (PBM) is what he has become, but he need not remain perfect unless he so chooses. For instance, his status can be a personal choice. Yes, some are forcefully enlisted through personally set calamities. Finally, the remaining cohorts are born into an initially inescapable trap; by the fate of birth in the wrong place and at the wrong time. Yet, here is an alternative view.

Any investigation of the PBM, alone, will not change his position in the American society. Only he can truly and completely change, who and what he is to himself and in the eyes of the world. Ultimately, it is his responsibility to abandon being The Perfect Black Man. Or, he can live all his days as a jester, full of obligatory misery to entertain needy, score hungry members of Club Schadenfreude.

Yet, contrary to popularized beliefs, which justify his plight, he does not deserve his situation. The notion that he "deserves" his position in life represents a very self-serving myth. What happens to The Perfect Black Man is highlighted in the searching questions embedded in the materials found in Books One, Two and Three of this series: **Escaping The Box**.

If the reader is in search of "solutions" for the Perfect Black Man; he or she should sit down and talk with a living, human profile, who fits their interpretations and perspectives of a PBM. Find the solution through a personal contact. Actually, make sure it is eye-to-eye.

About Soul Rot

It represents thoughts you can choose to feel after reading the books, in part or completely. Soul Rot is also a compendium of condensed perspectives in how and what people think about others. Those observations range from individuals' expressed feelings on people in their inner circles; employees compacted within their spheres of influence; and from their viewpoints of humanity, in general.

Of course, there are people who have no feelings about anyone other than themselves, including having no feelings about their own children.

The Perfect Black Man: Who and what is he?

Friends, family and others can help him make the platforms for transitions he desperately needs. More importantly are those key individuals, who help him disconnect from one world and overcome another. But, his "overcoming" isn't the action professed in the Gospel hymn. Instead, he will have to prevail over the expectations he has absorbed from the shell of his immediate world. The shell gives structure to where he finds many superficial, life requirements, which are transfused through powerful, and addictive behaviors.

They include, but are not limited to: a) continually practicing to not achieve; b) beliefs that he is not smart enough for the world; and c) engaging a so-called "**Plan,**" where he is kept as a *self-righteous slave to the memory of slavery.* All-the-while, and unknown to him, it is set to enrich others and impoverish him morally, physically, spiritually, intellectually, and financially-- forever.

Thus, his world is organized for him to believe he is stupid and cannot compete with all other people in the world. Of course, when he does see one of "his kind" making it in and beyond school; he surmises it is because that person is an athlete, screen entertainer or a real-life professional type—all escapees. They found door number **Six.**

For the uninspired and incurious, Door #6 is a mysterious and potential escape door from the PBM's six-sided world. He sees events, lifestyles, prestige, professional respect, **earned** by others in the world. He "knows" he cannot begin to think about them. Because he feels no one believes he is competent to become someone greater than he is today. He has no powers to earn anything outside of the street and his "world."

If he did become successful, through escaping from the box, then what does that say about his detractors and those perennial naysayers? What does it say about the people who make their life purposes to keep him in the box? What becomes of them, if he achieves greatness through escaping—without them in tow? What will they tell him he owes them? Then what will he believe he owes them, for what they think they have done for him? I just thought I would ask?

Driving through urban neighborhoods, you see young men, whose abandonment of addictive habits: could close prisons; sweep-clean, crime littered streets, and become honest, productive, supportive fathers and husbands. Unfortunately, many will attest they cannot see that vision of themselves.

I believe our society wants and even needs Perfect Black Men. Even though our economy needs creative entrepreneurs, skilled craftsmen, and global business people, etc. We need and want The Perfect Black Man more, recall the –"The Willie Horton." types.

We, being Americans and specifically Black Americans, need to continue developing young Black men. They must be made dependent upon Black America romanticizing real and fictive histories. All the while, we actively popularize retreating from the edge of an expanding Abyss called-- Success.

For example, Black America is constantly misrepresenting itself on TV, and in fashionable newspaper reports. Unfortunately, it is more like a religious experience in recycling beliefs, attitudes and self-limiting behaviors, condemned long ago as follies for fools.

In contrast, where are the sustainable economic, financial, technological, agricultural, manufacturing and scientific developments hiding? Who hid them away from the youth? Less we choose to forget, didn't the Civil Rights movements lay down layers of opportunities; from which **the future**, our youth, could learn and master? Again, who hid them away and for what reasons? Did we and I mean WE, condemn **the future** to create their own legacies of ignorance and errors of omissions?

Were we so threatened by what they could achieve, that we quietly aborted teaching them, formally and informally, concepts like: "responsibility;" "genius;" "mastering;" "achievement;" "self-respect;" and a host of other basic concepts? Did we conveniently delete success from their life vocabularies? I can imagine seeing a critical mass of "us," deciding to tell them, "We are not going to let you have something, we did not have!"

My one answer to all of those questions: **YES!**

We failed the future, by making them fail for us, to our satisfaction! And, now we visibly cry, while laughing in silence, over their collective miseries of short-comings, to become our "lost generations." We made it. Let's laugh at their misery.

Yes! We wanted them to fail!
Hey Black America, have you no shame?

What does the merging of mixed and contradictory messages inspire our youth to achieve?

—

6

I another light, I believe we have created a co-dependency between older, Black Americans and their surrogate offspring and alter egos, known as the PBM's. In turn, we have taught a few young and older men to direct their highest priorities on making themselves, "stupid." By embracing a culture, which favors ignorance over knowledge about the world. Then credits them for doing nothing positive with their lives. Of course, I could be wrong in this assessment. Doing nothing may actually be viewed by a few as a positive outcome.

Back to youth and messages

The images give them assurances, like below waist, underwear dominant baggy pants, the Perfect Black Man, should never feel out of place and unneeded. Again, The Perfect Black Man is a bedrock social commodity for America, or so we are led to believe.

Dr., MR., Mrs. and Ms, please ask yourselves, "Do you personally need the Perfect Black Man? If not, then why do others seem to need him? What services does he provide your neighborhood, community, local TV news groups, newspapers, schools, colleges, institutions, governments, churches, and politicians?" Don't sell yourselves short, by applying stereotypical responses.

Please answer the question:
Do you personally need the Perfect Black Man?

If you have a genuine soul, look into the depths of your feelings, deeper than fear—itself.
Face the question!

I believe there you will find why some Black, White and other

people **need**

The Perfect Black Man.

Then ask yourself, what does The Perfect Black Man need, which makes him the right partner in this long, ultimately corrosive social/relational venture? What gains enrich his life from this experience, from birth thru death?

Please look through the material in the books, selectively. Discover selections, which catch your attention and interests. Shock yourself! Think about the content: what is expressed and not expressed.

If you are a critical thinker, ask yourself about what would happen if the scenes expressed in the stories, etc., were to change or disappear? What would happen to The Perfect Black Man and to America?

What would happen to: the **social service industry,** to public schools, as they exist today, to America's standing in the global business world, and to the military? Then add **the prison industry,** and many other special interests and PAC groups, dependent upon The Perfect Black Man.

Don't forget to include the news and sports media: those which are real or pretentious or (fraudulent----your modern, popular snake oil, and carpet bagging types.)

I wonder if private companies would sprout up to serve as the public's support services to care for the PBM? Or in his absence, companies would appear to replace his services.

I can imagine a new category for special education services, which would classify the child version of the PBM as a **pre-Perfect Black Man.** Of course, there is precedence for this designation, as found in the form of **pre-delinquent children.** Is there overlap?

Can't you hear a teacher telling a matronly inquirer, that she teaches Pre-PBM's. The inquirer responds, "Oh, that must be so rewarding!" As the classification is prescribed to a mere child, will it reserve a spot for him in a system, already pre-disposed to treat him as permanently damaged goods? In essence, we would officially declare that he is: intelligently-ungiftable and Mission-education/Impossible. You pick—You be the judge!

My three books will provide you with only perspectives and interpretations. Do not anticipate finding solutions to something, which is not, by itself, a problem.

The Perfect Black Man represents a set of paradoxes. Each potentially includes contributions from every man, woman and child in America.

Relax and save your mental energies and faculties. You will have to go deeper than your soul to find the WILL to discover or create the solutions. Oh yes, remember to meet a living PBM. Then look for his counterparts in other groups. They are all around you.

Thank you,
Michael Mason Norman, ED.D.
March, 2011

A special note

The Denial Syndrome: Remember Congress, The White House, State Capitals, political parties, and CEO's, do not have practical answers for this set of paradoxes. What solutions can be found will require the focused attention and perspiration created among millions of people. They will need to unselfishly forward set their thinking for the good of the country. Why? The PBM represents a living variation of an open-sourced theme. The theme is now available among other Perfect_____ Men in America.

A key question: Will America continue burying itself in denial of what it sees everyday? The answer represents a solution for the whole "Perfect_____Man 3D game.

Our need for inventive, entrepreneurial, productive, intelligent, curious, courageous and aspiring young men; will only be satisfied, effectively, through how we treat them as intelligent and valued human beings.

Today we prefer: dumping them by the thousands into canyon size graves of confusion and pity; incarcerating thousands more to remove them from our feeble mind's eye. Afterwards, letting the strong waste away in workless lives, where they can set themselves free.

These are not viable options worthy of a great nation. It would be expected of a selfish, hubristic and inwardly driven people. If we add self-deceiving, we convert them quickly into an anti-humanitarian country. Like the one America had to overcome during World War II: a country which perfected ***Mass, Schadenfreude.***

What is America becoming?

It may be regressing into a face-saving and imaginary past, where fear shelters the insecure and truly scared. Not surprisingly, the first casualty of a regressive society is a progressive society. A progressive America champions entrepreneurial ambitions and inventive dreams, which strive to create better tomorrows. Those dreams will far exceed all those ever known to earlier generations.

So let me ask, what do you think are some of the other casualties, including collaterals, of a regressive society?

You -- Be The Judge.

Why The Perfect Black Man?

Article excerpt: Dr. Jonathan Theodore Kobayashi[1]

It was raining and I felt sick to my stomach about the Internet news alert stretched across the screen. It read, "Five young Black men found dead in a house." The house was just a few blocks away from where I lived during my teens. Everyday it seems something like this happens. "Why?" I thought for a long moment looking out into the grayness of my tree-lined street. It was November.

The accompanying story read too true. It was a matter of fact story, cold, deliberate and with no details wasted. The editing was clean, crisp and perfect to sell absolute gore -- absolutely. Gruesome lines told of their lives' terminal event: each head took five shots from a nine millimeter. "It was meticulous slaughter." What else could add to that, I could not say. The timing of the story was too coincidental to believe, as my final study on the lives of young black men was beginning the next day, November 25, 2024.

Yes, their deaths were brutal and closed. Now their bodies chilled in the City Morgue. I didn't finish the story because it was predictable; like a script from a TV cops and robbers drama. It was just the evening news was it not? More bodies, more stiff dead bodies, and soon forever forgotten lives. What kind of living leads someone to such a horrific end? All I could do was ponder that thought round and round in my head. I blanked the screen, but I could not blank the thought and images from my mind.

I pressed save and stored the story in my reading glasses.

---

[1] As you read this article, please check your vanity at the door of your mind. Dr. Kobayashi is a composite personality derived from thousands of people, who truly care about the world. If you know someone like this you are lucky. If you think it is written specifically about you, I must tell you that I don't know you.

Why were so many young Black men dying such horrible deaths? It seems life was not theirs to live. What a pity or is pity an inappropriate disclaimer? Perhaps we should blame them for staging their sudden, methodical termination on this earth? They deserved it for it was their Will! Some might suggest that comforting conclusion.

I suspended the thoughts, as growing frustration kept hammering and flattening each word. Thoughts were folding the question over and over, tempering each syllable, until I noticed I was creating a harder future for my study.

My feelings were forming into something different and now I was becoming a tool to attack the senseless slaughter. Letting my emotions take over reason for but a moment, I wanted to use my study as a weapon against wholesale manslaughter. For just that short period of time, I thought about how those young men were perfectly dead. Suddenly, a title found its place in my thoughts. I decided to call the study: The Perfect Black Man: How is he created, maintained and terminated at *Will or for Cause*?

Entering my thought space, the wall lights adjusted, automatically, for work. I activated my customized wrap-around 120 inch by 80 inch screen. It made the room turn a pale blue. I stood back from the surface (I like to write and read while standing at the four foot writing podium.)

Did I actually want to destroy someone, or did I want to destroy something? This was my real question.

My thoughts switched to a deeper feeling, more reflective as the moments passed, that I could no longer deny: those and other young men died meaningless, deaths because their lives were without meaning. Perhaps their lives were without meaning not only to themselves, but to others in their worlds' as well. What were their options?

For a moment, I thought simply, like the cheap, thought-free TV programs still in reruns from the Post-Iraq\Iran Dillusional years. It has been twelve years since the truth behind the Iraq war was exposed. Like Watergate long before, all hell broke loose. America discovered how dumb it had lived in the immediate post 9/11 years of war, amid confusion and self-doubt. Like Viet Nam, we were shrouded in the fog of impenetrable brain deadening lies. We learned nothing!

But back to today's ever present realities. We live in a place where lies die at the doors of honest people. Dumb-founded, lies, PACs and members of Club Schadenfreude, turn away-- unwelcomed.

Fantasizing, I wondered if I could discover one, easy answer to this trove of paradoxes. Of course, I knew better. As I pondered over the challenge, I reminded myself that human history is based upon complexities of actions, miscalculations and follies. All of which are far beyond any patience and curiosities of most beings. This is America. We have the emotional attention spans of an ice cube in a fire. As a teacher of adults, I know too well, that patience and curiosity went out of favor with most Americans over three decades ago. For the record, we faked having patience for another twenty years.

We scientist and historian types, still marvel how so many people collectively dropped, any interest in learning about multi-complex problems. They willfully abandoned critical thinking and sought to find one answer to explain any and all problems. They scavenged the land to source an immortal's home, which hides the holy silver bullet. It is a bullet, which can capture a better tomorrow for its owner.

But the next, best thing was created through consumption of a regular TV diet. Obesity of mind finally caught up with obesity of body. Millions found their very own Shangrila. It was delivered overnight to their homes. Yes, the lowly couch rose to become the holiest spot in a home.

Despite abundant CDC reports, there have been several holy silver bullet prescriptos. Shamelessly , they professed to know where the bullet was and is still hidden. Needless to say, they have made millions of dollars off of fools, who want the one answer to all their problems. Then and now they treat the prescriptos, as if they are messengers straight from silver heaven.

Woo! Ok, I am back to reality. That always leaves me feeling like I have slammed a dose of nightmare wine.

Again, thinking of the dead ones in the Morgue

I could only imagine that someone really cried for them. Of course, there will be many attending their funerals; but where were these people while they were alive? Or, I suppose I am just too disconnected from that world. I cannot understand what life has become for young men, who, through recent events, checked themselves into the City Morgue.

Our temporary residents in the Morgue are from so-called Black, African America communities. These are heavy residential--light commercial collections of a self-styled culture deeply at odds with itself. From my outside perspectives, some of the residents embrace this culture and live high on a philosophy of being victims.

Another part exist in limbo, adhering to beliefs that they can make it on their own. Yet, they realize they are perpetually uncertain in how and when to connect with the future. These individuals comfort themselves, while fearing the uncertainties of tomorrow. They live in the anonymity of the memories of strangers.

A final group stands alone, set quietly adrift from the lands of fatalists. This cohort is visible in a majority of the world's neighborhoods.

They or their parents learned haunting lessons through lifting and tossing away, the weights of self-pity from their shoulders. Those actions followed a deep realization that they and no one else, were responsible for their lives. Their eyes and minds focused on the future and how they would reach their goals in life. If they sought help, they knew they had to earn it, before receiving even a kernel of advice.

This cast of players was in constant reality therapy; never letting themselves feel contained by anyone or any part of the world.

Not surprisingly, contentment was placed at the bottom of a list of needs in their lives. Correspondingly, their biggest fear was in not trying to make it in the world; the larger world outside of where they lived, and outside of themselves. For them to not try was not an option. For them failure was colored the hue of not trying to live the best lives imaginable. They knew that hope and dreams were earned and not given as charity.

Somewhere in their worldly histories, they were made well aware of aspiration. Mindful of life's other options, they took to heart a necessity to achieve and not hide away from tomorrow. In contrast to today, progress was an emotional investment. It was and still can be a human quality, which they would never deny themselves, nor any of their generations to follow.

Ironically and as amazingly, these were Black Americans from another time. They were from an era, long before victimhood became institutionalized

Unlike members of the other groups, they disciplined their souls to build mountains and not just marvel at them from afar. Interestingly, these mates were not seeking views from the tops of mountains, not even the ones they built. Instead, they built peaks inside their hearts, minds and souls.

It was in those hidden spaces, were strength of purpose and being were enabled. In those quiet, personal spaces neither fear nor doubt overcame a silent pact with the future.

Roots die without leaves

Members of future oriented groups understood risks. Each understood and assumed some risks in moving far from their physical and emotional surroundings. It was a given at the time that such actions were expected from their families and peers. To move away, inevitably meant being touted as a turn-coat or worse yet, someone who had "sold out" by never going back to their past.

Sell-outs? Sell-outs to the future! I believe yes. In comparison, their nay-sayer's , who also double as no doers, sell themselves to every negative image about the world and themselves they can find. If they cannot find it, they seem oddly skilled and willful in creating new pasts and negative tomorrow's faster than memories are able to store them. If only that energy and creativity could be applied to making contributions for tomorrow. I only wish....For now that thought would just remain -- a thought.

Once my emotional state regained its calm and direction, I began to settle down and think more directly and coldly about this issue. The problem was not the bodies. The bodies personified a set of symptoms of something deeper, happening among several communities—titled by business, media and governmental and social service groups, as "the Black community."

(A side note: there is no real Black community: they are just neighborhoods where a lot of Black folks live. They may look like communities. Observe: community is the first misnomer you recognize, when you walk down the streets.)

"Black folk just love to live in illusions."

As my Black friends are always compelled to remind me. That is a lot when I become frustrated with some of their attitudes. Their favorite expression to recite:

"You know how we are! We are always just trying to get over on someone! We often work very hard to get over on ourselves too."

Excerpt: J. T. Kobayashi
Permission provided for inclusion
in Soul Rot

For Dr. Michael Mason Norman, ED.D.

A note someone placed under my office door:

Black America used to build its communities through building individuals. Now, it has become efficient at destroying itself, from within, by systematically preparing each child to destroy his adulthood, while he is still a child in mind.

Of course, a little help is needed to guide the child along. Much of that guidance comes from both the usual and surprisingly unusual suspects. Perhaps even from you! -- Anonymous

Chapter One: The Perfect Black Man

Image Capsule Diary

Looking back on 2010, I was forced to recall many of the preoccupations my friends and I had about being Black Men. We were angry back then. Why we couldn't see what our anger was about still amazes me; but yes, we were truly angry. All we had around us was the world and the world owed us, so much. Yet, unfortunately for the world, it didn't know how much it owed us, for we were born in America. America could never owe us enough, so we thought.

I know you appreciate that we were not like those foreign born black people, some of whom you might be tempted to call black. They have never come up to our more developed lives, not then, nor even now. But let me stay with "back then."

We had those special kind of Black Men back then. They were extraordinary, for some people actually called them *PERFECT*. The "perfect specimen," I recall one old fart news anchor person calling them, on what was then modern television. We no longer have need of those kinds of news people. Now, news is known, instantly, all around the world, if you want to know it.

That was true back then, but our "boys," they liked to be called boys back then too; well, hear me, they just stepped out on the streets in whatever clothes they needed to be seen in and just presented themselves to the world. They were the news in the neighborhood.

Perfection doesn't need to be reported. Me and my homeboys were the most perfect Black men on the earth. We were too clean to be seen on the scene. We were so perfect that even mirrors couldn't reflect our presence and souls.

Flash, dash, stash and cash-only, were our calling cards; as we made noise without opening our mouths. We simply looked louder than our surroundings. You know! Ah, you do know, I mean, don't you?

The game was "image this!" That was all we had then and that is all our namesakes have today to call lives. Back then, most did not work, for they just didn't know how to take care of themselves. Today, we are still "kept men." By standards set long ago, you aren't anyone if someone isn't taking care of you -- everyday.

No self-respecting Black man would dare admit that he really took care of himself, without a lot of outside support. Someone once told me that I was truly disrespectful of my grandmother, because she always took care of me. I slapped him silly for talking about my grandmother like that. He deserved worse, but fools need compassion too. Of course, he didn't know what he was talking about. You have to be a Black man to really understand, what life was like then and what it has become today.

Look at me! I am perfect in every way. People need me and they practically fall over one another to take care of me. Look at them out there, looking at me! I must be pretty, the way they look at me? I know they want to own me and take me home with them.

I don't have to work. I don't have to do nothing. Life is E A S Y. That is why it is always easy money. Forget the hope and dreams junk. You have to work when you have Hope and dreams, you know?

Look, look what do they see? All they see is my perfection and they truly want me to stay this way. So I stay this way, how cool is that? **TOO COOL!**

The Sermon from the CHAIR

Recorded: It is 2025, your town, your neighborhood, your barbershop.
GPS location: a barbershop in a native born, African-American neighborhood.
NEXT: I am visiting and I need a haircut. Sitting down: I am sitting across from a row of three barber chairs. Each is occupied.

I can see myself in the mirrors behind the chairs. Man, am I conspicuous! I think I have a long wait, but I need the haircut and I have no appointments this afternoon. Of course, it won't be a waste of time. I always like to pick up some of the local spirit in any new town and this will work very well. How well? Uh, that remained to be seen. But patience has always been my friend; as waiting is always priceless in my work.

Looking around

It is a mixed aged group. The talk is quiet, with limited jiving. That is unfortunate! I don't hear talk like that, as much as I used to and I miss it. "They talk funny where I live." Just joking to myself. Such are the consequences of my work and acquired lifestyles.

Good! People seem respectful of one another. That is a good sign. I hope it last during my stay in the room of strangers. But then again, a little excitement is great for a seventy-five year old, going on fifty.

Suddenly, the speaker and his speech or could it be, a sermon began. No one seemed surprised, as I came to appreciate why, a little later. So I acted like the others and just went with the flow. Again, patience, my old friend, came to the rescue and on cue, reminded me to just hang loose.

"Gentlemen, please look at this crowd before me." The speaker was sitting in the middle chair, directly in front of me. All the other seats were taken, so I was the center of his cold, star like black-eyed peas gaze. I looked over him quickly. I saw nothing alarming for the place and time. So I returned to my ebook in my reading glasses. I was just starting to read a section I needed for work.

The Show began

He was tall, with a black barber's sheet draped over his chest and down to his knees; although I couldn't quite make out how he was dressed. So, I continued my focus, ever so casually, on his head. It was a head I would never forget.

His eyes were deep, dark and mysterious for a man, by estimate, about 45 years of age. The most striking feature of his head was his 19th century, impressionistic "Moses-like" beard. It was as white as fresh mountain powder, against a deep contrast of a day-break blue in the morning. The beard, strangled his mouth, as it ran down from his upper lip, to at least eight inches below his chin and as wide. The combination, along with his skin tone, spelled intimidation. Even for a gold-weighted Knight from SomewhereLand!

Now to his voice.

When he first spoke I heard a fearless resonance, which bounced among the walls of the shop for a long, but tension filled, reverb moment. Here was a man accustomed to not needing an amplification system. For a moment, I sensed a show was approaching. How brilliant I am every so often, and this was one of those so often moments. *Ok, it was a lucky call. Hey I am honest!*

Finally, the barber pulled the sheet from around the neck of the speaker. The move exposed a shock and awe display of colors. There, amazing! Look at those rings upon rings of brilliantly shinny, gold chains, reaching from his neck to his belt.

His shirt could blind a peacock. So distracting was the display I just gave up reading. It was the show within a show. I could not ignore the display of hues and sun-like shimmers of gold distorting the images in my glasses. The words and graphics simply disappeared. Perhaps this would really create a new experience for me? It was just a question, nothing more at that moment. A show? Yes!

I put the glasses away and put on my shades. That was better, now I could see again. I looked around and others had joined in putting in darker "eyes" to shade the x-flaring, radiating view – front and center.

I thought: *Earth to Sun: Warning sun! Warning sun! Human competition on earth.* Warning! *The leaves of the plants were turning his way.* Never before had I witnessed a human being creating phototropism with his presence. Amazing!

The sudden transformation from a simple client in the chair to a Benin like king, made the space between us feel warm and surreal. The weight of the metal around his neck moved my feeling, into sensing the presence of a tribal council meeting.

So it began, a rare spectacle for me: a sermon was commencing, not from a mountain top, nor from a stage, but from a barber's chair. The room fell quiet, even reverent in silence. All that was missing was a choir in the background, vocally shadowing each word of the speaker.

But this man could not tolerate upstaging. He took a deep breadth and inhaled all of the living spirit in the room. Then he released all that was in his lungs! Heaven have greater mercy upon us.

His breadth was morbid and distilled.

He was the sermon and music need not apply to provide background support. Side note: I am still glad Ray Charles had his singers and band.

Unbeknownst to all, my shades had a commercial set of stereo-microphones supported by one terra-byte of space for audio and video. The shades were cameras in Super 3DHD. It is the latest, greatest recording system on the market for my kind of work. Yes, I began recording something that could not be left to a, "You should have been there!" tale. Fishing stories are all lies (not mine of course,) but this was the truth and it needed witnessing.

I sat straight faced, motionless and aware of the piercing eyes looking at me. They were those of one barber I had been recommended to meet and have him cut my hair. He motioned for me to come up and have my haircut to order. I waved him off, and suggested he let a family of three boys and a father proceed in front of me. I just wanted the time to unfold, while I was sitting in the path of the sermon. The barber knew my game and skipped me. The father said thank you.

I really wanted to know what those boys were thinking? If I had been their ages, what would I have thought of the scene?

I was prepared for either the sermon to lift me, into heaven or leave me rolling on the floor. There I would beg for death to stop the side splitting pain of laughter. Now the inner voice, which counseled me to show a little more respect, pulled hard on my left ear. I accepted the advice, but barely!

The sermon blows (You can hear it in stereo, if you let your imagination fixate upon the possible. Place yourself in a rough-domed theater with perfect acoustics. Sit back and just think you are listening to a speech, given by some one, perched in his own heaven.)

The Sermon Begins!

"Hear me my friends."

He speaks clearly and looks down from his stealthy place on the edge of the Chair. For the moment I am the focus of his attention. Of course, I am compelled to stare back in respectful reverence, for he commands the room. *I will let the speaker continue, without my editorial interruptions. You wish!*

"Hear me my friends, my brothers, ah my brothers, heal thy selves!"

With a slow deliberate panning of his head, he looked into each man's eyes. Without hesitation, he just looked and kept talking as he scanned the audience of fourteen souls.

When he reached the three boys, our master of the sermon took an extra second to look into each eye. Now satisfied they were fully mesmerized, he continued his scanning. The father of the boys was sitting with his eyes closed.

This was his congregation for the hour, as he had ordered up the full works, to reserve uninterrupted time for his complete version of Sermon "X".0. Both of us were getting the full works.

"My brothers, my brothers, do you not see who you are, who we are? We are the children of a land far away and we need to return to that land to find ourselves."

His arms started swinging too and fro, while the barber took extra care to not interfere with the orchestration of the speech. He kept cutting away below the chin and down to the speaker's skin. It was a shave job and before us began an amazing transformation.

The speaker stopped to look over his shoulder at the presence in the mirror. Satisfied, he returned to his sermon from the Chair.

"My brothers aren't you feeling what I feel and see what I see? We need to go back to where we belong far from here. I do miss it, I can feel it in my bones, the air is still in my lungs and I need to return to my home place. Will you join me?"

As if on cue, a voice softly rose from a corner near the door. He asked, "Where are we suppose to go and where have you been?"

The preacher looked undisturbed by the intrusion and kept swinging his arms. His eyes began to roll around, separately. One turned clockwise, while the other revolved counter-clockwise. Yes, I did see that!

I felt my mouth caving in. It was bone dry. I couldn't swallow. My jaw was getting extremely heavy. The floor beckoned me to join it. To embrace it, square foot by square foot! I could imagine that there I might find my only relief, from my growing sense of torture. My breathing you wonder? Oh yes, I forgot to breath. Ha, I was holding my breadth. Not good!

All my ribs were cracking under the strain. My restrained laughter index was shaking uncontrollably. The meter read in my glasses, "you are off the charts......seek medical attention...you are entering hysterical sphere!" Immediately, the "off the charts" message pulsated warnings. Suddenly I heard an audible in my ear piece: "Seek immediate medical relief! Do you need an ambulance? Next of kin will be notified in one hour, mark count, 59 minutes."

He kept on talking, it sound more like he was humming to himself for a moment, then the sermon returned after a brief intermission.

"My brothers look at yourselves can you see what I see in your minds? I see nothing in you for you have nothing to offer the future. All you have is your pathetic, individual pasts.

"My brothers look at me. Look at me! I am the reason we need to go back, look what I have become and you can become this way yourselves. I am the wonder of wonderful! The bread was inspired by me!" On those words he stood, raising his hands, reaching for the ceiling. The ceiling fan nearly clipped off his fingers. Checked by technology, unable to ascend into heaven, he returned to his earthly urbanized, majestic throne.

The young men in the room started laughing out loud at the living spirit figure in the Chair. The three boys did not utter a sound, but simply studied the gentleman more closely than could I.

Curious?

As others sat gainfully entertained, I started surveying his clothing and regalia of gold chains. Studying him became my therapy from the pain. I asked myself, "Who was this guy and why was he trying to convert the inconvertible to something unknown?" Ok, that was an editorial, I slipped, please excuse me, I always ask questions. It is my critical nature.

Again patience
It tries to counsel, but even the voice of patience is starting to shake and quiver. I think I am in a race with my adviser to be the first on the floor. But not yet, there is more to come. The sermon is yet young.

"Don't you see yourselves in the mirror behind me! Blind have you become by your foolishness and dreams of glory beyond what you can see. I don't want to be like you young men, you are young men are you not?"

The feet started rustling and the barber to my left motioned for the crew to just stay cool and to spare themselves. To steal away would have been their loss. Obviously, he knew the routine and was well prepared to intervene -- if necessary.

"My young brothers I see you and you see me, but there is more to me than I see in you. Do your mothers know where you are right now? What lies have you told them today about how you are living your lies and how you will make them proud of you? I am not talking about the mothers who raised you. I am talking about the women, those girl figures whom you call on your cell phones, to just to let them keep tabs on your activities. And they have to keep tabs on your acts, for they cannot trust your sorry selves one hot Detroit minute west of Chicago."

Someone must be from Detroit as he begins moving for the door. With impeccable timing, as soon as he reaches for the handle, a police squad car passes by. It stops. An officer begins peering through the shop windows. The young man brakes, and turns about face. Quickly he backtracks to his chair. Surprisingly, he is suddenly disinterested in leaving for the silence of the street outside.

Another curiosity.

The three boys have not moved, nor said a word to one another.
The speaker's barber stops to take a call.

He tries to do his work and talk at the same time, but his wife is talking trash to him about something. He is obviously frustrated with her language. We can hear her from a distance and those words will not be repeated to protect the barber's image. But we did cover our ears, out of signaling empathy for his tongue lashing. Personally, I was expecting her to walk through the door. No, walking is too slow. She would have been stepping fast, while melting his phone in his hand. For the rest of us, the order of the moment would have started and ended with the words: "Get the hell out of here!"

The Speaker
"My brother Mr. Barber, can't you tame that lady? I mean you know who is boss in this world and it ain't you."

"Ouch!" I could think of no other response, for I felt sorry for the barber.

The speaker makes a solo laugh. No one is tempted to join his slam against someone with a razor in his hand. The barber ignores him and keeps about his business on the lines around the speaker's neck. I am tempted to start a chant: cut him, cut him, cut him. But that would ruin my objectiveness, would it not?

"My brother men, trip over yourselves to touch me. I am too pretty for you to only look at. You must touch my royal likeness." The speaker rose and toured the room. No one touched him. Pity!

The barber has finished his work and the timing couldn't have been better. For my time was starting to run out. My seat was opening soon. Shame, shame, what a show! The pain is receding, the warnings have stopped and the count died.

I wondered about the name of the speaker, as he started putting on his coat over his weighted down body. It was summer (80 degrees F.) I caught his glance and took advantage of the opportunity.

"My brother." I spoke slowly so not to alarm him. He looked up and studied my non-street looking self. He measured my voice for either sarcasm or fear. Then he narrowed his shoulders and stepped towards me. I wasn't sure what to expect: a hug, a slug, a tackle, or a prolonged stare-down. The barber waiting to cut my hair came from around his chair, but didn't approach us.

The speaker reacted to my words, " My name is My Brother!" He sneered with the "r" and just stared my way, through me it seemed, as he walked pass and out the door in full regalia. No entourage joined him. Another shame.

He looked at the policeman still parked in the middle of the street. The officer just shook his head and laughed out loud and drove on. I guess he had enough of the show, even for a Black policeman, watching an old White guy acting like a Black, African king. Amusing, yes amusing.

After My Brother had left, the room tried to go back to normal. But it was impossible until a change of players had completed the transfusion of bodies over the course of an hour. None of them seemed stunned, but a few did seem unsettled by the experience.

Who was this guy who definitely did not fit into their world. Yet the speaker was talking about them with impunity? If this guy had been their age or looked like them, they would have dragged his specialness out on the street. Once there they would have beat a new memory and value for life into him; very economically and age neutral, by the way.

Odd, I sensed, for it felt they tolerated his weird behavior, odd indeed. Or was it really odd? Had odd become normal and normal had become odd?

I wondered if I would ever see My Brother again or would he, like so many others I have encountered during my research, simply disappear? Where was the place he wanted us to go? That I learned soon afterwards.

Upon inquiring, a policeman, who knew him from the street, told me that he had placed My Brother in jail more times than anyone knew how to count. My Brother loved jails, they were his home and he felt that is where those young men in the barbershop belonged.

He went around preaching about going to jail and made it sound like the promised land. Is this another message young men are hearing from the street? Do they have enough sense to not hear it and not listen to its messengers? Do they have enough sense to run away from the speakers of personal apocalypse? Yet, perhaps others need to hear such a speech from the likes of My Brother. That is a very curious thought.

Now, what did those three little boys hear? JTK.
Somewhereland, 2025

Chapter Two: There are no "gaps!"

Why We Die So Young

When I first saw Tyronne he was walking with his posse. They swayed slowly in their new deep-dropping and "full-like" diaper denims. If they had to move quickly (like run), they were doomed after one step. They often overlook that fact: oversized and unbelted pants drop off waists, once hands are removed. Down to their ankles goes everything, including oversized underwear. Yes, it is an embarrassing moment, even when the laughs subside.

As they approached me they all stared straight ahead or downward, except Tyronne. He alone chose to look me in the eyes. He didn't blink his green eyes! I later recorded his attire and fashion styled "attitude."

He seemed different from the others he accompanied. His clothes were cleaner and seemed more critical of himself in how he looked to the outside world. Upon first impression, he wasn't trying to take fashion too seriously, but was more inclined to try to show pride in himself, non-verbally.

Thinking back on his glance into my eyes reminded me more of people in the South. Some of them will look you in the eyes, while not afraid to say something as simple as a genuinely friendly "hello." Once again, I was reminded that the restricted world of young men on the streets of urban America are not so kind to hellos from strangers.

After reflecting upon the contrasting appearance of Tyronne to the others, I decided to interview him for my study on the self-recorded life expectancies of young men. The next day I searched for him along the block where I had first run into him. The street scene was sparse, as the sidewalks were abandoned. He was nowhere to be found.

Finally, during another follow-up trip, two days later, I spotted him. This time he was by himself and perhaps approachable—yet with the absence of the posse, he looked vulnerable too.

He saw me and seemed puzzled as I walked towards him. Standing not a fraction over six feet tall and weighing in around 165 pounds, he towered over my five-seven dumpy frame of super-sized, excess "skin" covered bones. I stopped him as we came closer and asked him if he had a moment to talk? He nodded a quick "ok". Then my interviewee glanced a 360 to see who was watching our exchange.

I described my ongoing project to him and asked if it would be ok for me to interview him? He thought about it for a couple seconds and then said, he had no problems with the idea. Tyronne qualified is response by specifying that we meet in a distant neighborhood, so people couldn't get into his business. *My note: street tactics* and reality.

The Interview

When we met the next day, about three miles away from where we first sized up one another, it was in a large coffee shop. To say it was upscale was an understatement. He bought his own health drink and I had to have a double "Expressed-so." To begin the talk I had to slowly warm up to him. I warned that I ask direct, sometimes blunt questions. He said go ahead! Tyronne continued saying he had nothing to hide and was interested in hearing the questions. He added that I should be prepared for blunt responses too.

He promised to treat me respectfully.

At this point I was beginning to wonder, who was I really talking to here: a street kid or someone with much keener and worldly attributes, hiding behind an official, wannabee rough veneer?

Note: He seemed curious about something, but why?

Consequently, given my demanding query, I decided to let him begin the interview, by having him ask me a couple questions.

First, he wanted to know what I was doing with my life, to have so much time walking around neighborhoods far away from my own?   I told him I was curious on how young men, like himself, were living during our recession? More specifically, I wanted to learn as much as possible, through interviews, on their educations and how they were helped or hurt by their educations?

Then he queried on what I could possibly learn from him? Both were reasonable questions. I responded that I wanted to talk with him, because he acted very differently from the others I had met.   He looked at me and laughed. "Hah," he said, "I don't live on the street." He went on to shake my confidence in my observation skills, by observing that my view of the world, was just a little on the extreme side of being out of date. I think he was suggesting that my line of questioning was making my career redundant. Of course, I needed some clarification on those last points.

Some Clarification

He checked my reasoning by highlighting that hanging out doesn't mean you are living on a particular street. With clearly articulated phrasing, he explained that like the coffee shop we were sitting in, the street can be a "Third Place" in your life.

As with many suburban kids who congregate in malls, etc., the street is the place for the less well off to come together and socialize with like-minded friends. But how safe was it for him to venture around on the streets? His response: "No more than it was for you my grand inquisitor!"

As a never been a gang member type, he had no deep connections or identity with any community sub-institution like a gang or even a local school. Since he wasn't a member of a gang, he was a free man and could go wherever he wanted in the world. Which is definitely not true for gang members. But I didn't buy his response on face value. So I hit him between the eyes. I wanted the truth about his gang membership?

I thought he was going to get up and leave, given the way he started adjusting himself in his seat. Instead, he just looked down at his hands and began moving his eyes to left field, then right. He was not happy to hear that question for info. on his earlier life. He let his body language do the protesting. The question ultimately prevailed.

Ever so tentatively, he sat back, then upright from his sag and leaning-to-just-this-side-of-hell style. Zooming in on me, with his now neon green electric eyes, he homed in, dead set into my pupils. At first, his street discipline searched for a reason to trust me: I was a stranger among strangers from outside his world. Mentally bolting forward, he suddenly opened up!

Once upon a time Tyronne belonged to a group, but he wouldn't tell me which one. Street protocol wouldn't let him go that far, nor reveal what he did as a member. Ok, that was enough to know. But, from here on the real interview had to move into quick step. If I didn't pursue more information right then, I might lose contact with him after that day. In my work a gamble is always about gambling for the right moment .

I shuffled my note cards. Glancing left, I noticed a clock hitting twelve bells, (noon.) Lunchtime was upon us. I asked him if he were hungry? He responded with an affirmative, but not with an American thumbs-up. Given there were several great restaurants in the block, I offered to buy him, his self-admittedly, first meal of the day. The place to eat was his choice.

Stepping out on the sidewalk, he looked up and down the block and saw an Indian storefront, listing Southern Indian cuisine. Yummy! That is what he chose because he had never eaten at one and I commented that it had an all-you-can eat buffet. He asked how I knew and I answered, well trust me, you will like it! But, did he like hot?

"Yes!" "OK, Perfect, you will live through the ordeal! Just live long enough to answer my questions." Jokingly, I commented, "hell hath no fury by fire, like really spicey, gratuitously hot Indian curry." His forehead started sweating, voluntarily. I thought to myself, "Food, makes the best torture. It is satisfying for all involved. Is it not so?"

So for the next three hours he gorged himself with plate after plate of chicken tandoori, rice, and mass amounts of other MORE insanely, mouth blisteringly--please let me die, hot foods. He was definitely a hungry wolf, with an untouchable-ice, cold palate. But, I wondered about the sensitivity of his stomach?

During his feast on stomach fire, he answered my questions and we both learned much from one another. Eventually, I had to back away from the table, as the spices made my eyes burn. Ok, some fool made me rube my eyes. That Dummy!

Earlier, when he started eating I sat back and searched his eyes to see if I could find honesty or find nothing? Finally, when he took a break and looked up from his plate, I pierced into those green eyes, deeply fixed within a Florentine chiseled, pre-sweat, unblemished, lightly brown stone colored face.

His skin reminded me of figures in rooms reserved for special statues of national, cultural heroes. For my uninitiated readers, those platforms are found in closely guarded areas of national wax museums.

(Where "touch and you die" rules apply. That is not a mere figure of speech in some places of the world. But held "untouchably" literal in its execution. In short, don't test what literal means, let alone the severity of the concept called: execution.

> *Remember: it is not always magic that can make a person disappear. Don't, <u>expletive deleted</u>!)*

Let us continue: closer spying on my uncovered and glutinous friend, exposed: his hair was cut close and razor lined around the front. The hair on the sides of his face was neatly lined as well. My interviewee's speech was clear, yet not slowed down to a reflective pace. Nonetheless, his words were studied before he made a statement. As our conversation progressed I began noticing his posture changing; becoming more upright, and the slouching had disappeared. I wondered to myself on whether he had become more relaxed for a moment?

Briefly, he looked as if he were maturing before my eyes. Now my questions became more demanding for introspection and reflection. I thought about whether or not he was ready to shed his adolescent fail-safe guard? A change in impression required a change in tactics.

Therefore, I shifted my thoughts back to the questions previously readied for the interview.

Tyronne, the adult

> *I asked him if I could superficially suspend him in a 3D, surreal space, normally confined for intelligent adults? That was a bad choice of words. I think I patronized him? Oops! You don't patronize adults! You did patronize him.*

But I felt he had to hear that I wanted him to think about himself: not at street level; but on the life platform for which he ultimately aspired. I was setting up a combination interview, with mentoring and counseling sessions as focused, add-on apps. Again, I was a step behind and again I was quickly earning redundancy points! Who was researching whom at this point? Oops! Oops! Double ooops! So, I will admit it, I am an Uber ooper!

As an interviewer, I didn't need to hear the "company line" from the street. Suddenly, he shed his more intimidating street persona. And, as quickly, he converged his speech and thought patterns into a bundle of urban street, hip-private school suburban teenager and the introspection of an intellectually-heavy college student.

Immediately and visibly, he was moving into his comfort zone and I could now see in his eyes, that my lunch partner could really think for himself. Still, how he ate like a pig at that buffet! I think he set an unofficial state record for human and beast consumption of food. I am glad we didn't try this at home.

Let me continue:
Contrary to my normal protocol, I am going to share with you, my notes from the interview. I have transcribed and made them G rated for any general audience.

The Interviewer's Notes
(Tyronne (Ty) is not his real name)

Interviewer: "Tyronne, from your time on the streets, what have you learned about what it means to be a man?"

Ty: "From what I can tell I am not suppose to be alive. Men and I, and I must tell you that some of us are only boys disguised as men, are not expecting to past twenty-five. If we go to jail, which most of my peers expect to do, we'll have already gone at least once before 22.

(Tyronne assured me he had not at this point in his life.) When you get out, you are reborn on the street. Isn't it funny how jail time might actually extend your life? Jail protects you from the realities of the outside. You have family (in jail), so I have heard. No one is going to let you starve; you just have to stay out of people's way. That's all. I think that is all!"

He went on.

"People who live on streets, and are young, are not expected to live like other people and I haven't seen too many examples of people living on or near street life, who actually have lives worth living."

"We are constantly being told that our lives are better on the street than in school or getting a so-called real job. My friends tell me that I am a king, while hanging with them and forget about doing anything "productive." He laughs at the term. "Actually I am exotic to them. Of course, you can see (why?)"

"Going productive is for chumps who have sold out. That is not to say that our heroes haven't sold out. You know which ones I mean don't you? When you look at those guys on the videos they have lives, worth living. They are real people! We see them on TV and in the movies. "

"They have submissive and oppressed women, cars, magnum cribs that can never end. Those boys in the hoops, just keep making baskets worth of money. Now that is living, but I can't do that. My friends can't do that either."

"'Who are we?' I always ask myself. Why won't we sell out and live like those normal people who are outsiders?"

"I can't afford to be a sell out because that would separate me from my friends and the rest of the people, who live around here you know." (A long pause)

"I can't leave them, what would that make me, who would I be to them and to myself? I can't see myself as an outsider." "Look at those outsiders, who are they fooling with their fancy educations, nice facades called homes, and trips around the world. Those bums live on the outside of real life. Look! I am an insider. School was a place to learn how to live like an outsider. No! I can't live like that, it would not be real and thus not me."

"Think about this for a moment Mr. Interviewer: if you think you are going to live for only a short amount of time; why, what do they call it, ah, ah, invent, no invest, yes that is right. Why invest in yourself by going to school. What a waste of time Mr. Interviewer."

" You always hear the statements that you have to think about how much money you can get if you get and education. Like getting a high school paper. How worthless, what a joke, I look around and see graduates washing dishes. I also hear college grads are not able to find jobs to pay off their college educations. I am going to live now and maybe, just maybe I will see 30."

"Yes, I think about these things, but I cannot say many of my street friends do. The women yes. Not all, but many for they have to think about how they are going to take care of their children. Especially when they don't want grandparents to have to take care of their children, as they were earlier in their lives."

"They know they have to get an education, for no real men are going stay around or even try to know such women. You know Mr. Interviewer, real men are outsiders. No matter what color, those who take care of their children and those who also have real jobs, are just chumps living on the outside of reality."

"We on the inside are privileged, not under-privileged. See that is the joke to us. The under-privileged are on the outside. On the other hand, the truly privileged, like us, are on the inside. Get it? We are protected from the dreadful things others have to live through."

"You do this interview stuff and it reminds me of a university research center, which or that went into my neighborhood not long ago. Where are the stores, the job making businesses? Now, Mr. Interviewer how will a research(er) center which looks at us help us? We are now a lobaroratory **(intentional spelling for his pronounciation)** for a few not real doctor types."

" Come to think of it, I am always amazed by the questions asked my friends about their lives. I am surprised how much outsiders know about us and how we live. You start to think that some of these people actually live around us."

"Then there are people, like you, who like to study us too. What could any of you really know about us?"

"In all honesty, Mr. Interviewer, I have studied you interviewer types and wonder if you see us as really special people? Off script: let me explain. Put down your note pad please and just listen. I hope you remember what I am going to say and don't interrupt, please dear sir."

Notes taken from memory

"I think we are special people, we must be given how much attention police, agencies, churches, governments, charities, and the news people spend trying to explain us to the outside world. Do you know how many different directions we are advised to take with our lives?"

"Go here, go there, no don't listen to them, we are the experts, listen to us. On and on and on the talk goes, under our feet, over our heads, it is just exhausting. It gets so exhausting you quit listening to people, who don't listen to themselves. Why listen to people who are afraid to listen to you?"

Suddenly, the speech stops. The restaurant is empty, but we just sit in the back as they prep for the evening dinner. No one asked us to leave.

Ty looks down at the card, which I turned to face him with a question typed on it. It says, "What does it mean to be a man?"

Shifting himself in his chair, he also seems to reposition his thoughts back to this particular question and away from his earlier observations.

"I have never known my father. I guess he is a man. I hope so. My mother doesn't talk about him, nor about any of the other characters she has hanged around with over my lifetime. The older people I know just seem to do their things around here and don't mess with us younger crowd. Some of them think we are the "lost generation." From what I can tell some of them come from another lost generation as well. What do you think Mr. Interviewer?"

I waited with no response. Impatient, he continued.

"Some go to church, why I don't know. It hasn't made them rich or anything beyond the Sunday clothes they wear one day a week. They aren't driving real cars. Some of them live in houses they own and their children live far from here; maybe suburbs I suppose. Who knows and my friends don't care. That is all like outside. But does all of that make the males men? Answer that for me Mr. Interviewer."

Not expecting a response from me, he again returns to where he left off.

"A man to me has money, women and flash and dash car that is lean, head high deep. Where we live you aren't living unless you are seen, in the right ways and times. You cannot see a diploma from a rinky-dink school. Otherwise, you aren't anything because you don't have anything and thus you are no one; no man so to speak."

"These kinds of men live real lives. No one is telling them what to do, or how to live. They hang with their own group and here they are."

"Real men don't have to do anything they don't want to do. They are 'cool' and that is with a big `C' too. Their acts are tight."

The Interviewer looks puzzled at Tyronne. So Ty feels sympathy for the interviewer, and thus compelled to add a little clarification to keep the pace going. He is on stage and in many ways he is scripting, directing and performing his life story for a one person audience.

Tyronne: "It means they have everything running in their favor. Their people, their games, their lives are all going well. No one messes with them and they are respected by all those around them. Respect is everything and I mean everything! Should I spell that for you? People listen to them, that is respect. At least that is how it works for those who do everything right."

"I can't say I am cool right now. I need to do a lot more things to get my own group of people around me, who respect me and make me the center of their lives. Again, like those with Entourages. Those are the real people."

"Can I tell you a little secret my dear Interviewer? The spaces between the insiders and outsiders are called the gaps. We must maintain those gaps at all costs. Part of it is image making and part of it is to help us create the circles for our extended entourage to form. I could call it a "circle of identities." It is like having an extended, distant fan club. So here is a more serious *p e r spec tive* on that little subject."

"We have a few around here who live a great life, with their own people. But not too many right now. Every once in a while the streets cleanse themselves of all comers and wannabee's. It is the change of life right before your eyes if they are alive to see."

"Life on the street is like that, where people just have to go as the property gets a little overcrowded or over priced and a few have to leave to make room for others."

Interviewer: "You mean some have to die?"

Tyronne: "Not really, but the police (the biggest gang in town and co-regulators, along with the courts over the street economy) help weed out those who just couldn't make it on the concrete, or got too big for the local action. They had to make for bigger space and as easily space was made for them in far away places; like hell for example, prisons and other cities. "

"Imaging what it would be like if all the thugs, including all those thugs in corporate suits, where still around. Obviously, there wouldn't be enough things to do and share among everyone. So, it is like a few people just disappear and are quickly forgotten, like those artists on the rap and music videos. Here today and puff/poof/like gone tomorrow specimen of yesterday. But, let me guess your next question: Why do I want to be part of this?"

"My answer is that I need to do something with my life and I can't see any other way to go. Selling out is not an option for me. That is an act of pure failure and there is no **cred** in losing to failure. Imagine you create an entourage, which is based on not failing through selling out."

"I need to make life easier, but it won't happen doing that stuff like you are doing. What would I do with that and what would happen to my people without me? They need me as the center of the entourage, its purpose and supplier of hope. There is no fun in working for a living, when you already have a living. I am a candle and my friends are moths."

"No, I just can't go out there where you outside people live. The gap is beyond meeting my needs. That wouldn't be right for this homeboy, it wouldn't be comfortable nor safe for me as well."

He pauses to look around to see who is near.
He clears his throat and expands his voice down an octave and softer.

"I don't think you know what it is like for people like me, who need to be with their own crowd. Young Black men, real African American males in your words, cannot do what the rest of the world does with their lives. We know poverty of spirit and ambition and power of fear and especially our brand of fear."

Another puzzled expression on the face of the interviewer.

"I mean we want to be feared by our women, by Whites, by Chinese, by Indians, by Mexicans, by everyone. Women are here to take care of us, that is a kind of natural law from our perspective. They need our power over them to make them feel wanted and loved. We are their children too. "

"When you have people believing you cannot take care of yourself, that you are children; they feel righteous in making sure you are kept a child. By doing so, you don't have to do anything for anyone other than yourself."

"Taking care of us makes you a Mission in the minds of some people, it can even become their calling in life. We dudes cannot take care of ourselves; so others volunteer their time and donate their money. Now that is making life easy. Can you hear all that easy money?"

Interviewer: But, like the slaves a century or so ago, doesn't that keep you in your place, including the women and others, who have to take care of you as well?

Tyronne: "I forgot to thank you for lunch. Next question please."

Anticipating that reaction, I moved on.

Interviewer: Why do so many young Black men die young?

Tyronne: "Why? Where have you been since I have been talking man? Ok, ok, ok, Ty will calm down and be civil like. We die young because life is so hard for us. You know we just aren't allowed to live like everyone else and that's why we are always set up to die before we have a chance to have a decent life. Now, it doesn't mean we actually die and get buried 6 below in the mud. It can mean we die and get buried among the living."

"That is what happens to many on the streets in this world, especially around here. I think it must be like that in other parts of the world, for that is what it is like around here."

"Yes, if it is bad here it must be that way else where too; except where people live on TV and in the movies. Those soap people and others all have it made. Look how much money they make!"

"Let me think about your question. Do I want to die while I am young? Well, if I do die young, I won't know what it means to live to be old, now will I?"

"There is no hope for me to live old any way. I look around and try to find old people who still have style. I don't see any of them having any fun in their lives. All they do is sit around and talk to one another. They watch the world drive by and shoot the breeze. In turn, life seems to just pass them by, every and I mean every day. You have seen them I am sure. You probably know them and I would strongly suggest you interview them as well. They stand on the corners passing time, like dogs sniffing one another."

"That is not what I want for my life as I move along into my twenties (he is 18). I am a player and players must do their things--right. Granted there are risks in being a player and you just can't afford to let life get you down. Players are cool and they don't really die. I would die if I went on in school. I can't imagine myself learning anything I already don't know. "

"You remember I said earlier that school and all that stuff is for chumps and chumps are not cool. Chumps always end up losing in life."

"The next time you want to interview someone, interview one of the dead head boys on the streets. You can spot one by how he looks, dresses and moves. They like to move quickly and go to school: look for the loaded down backpack and lack of a posse. They think they are smart and all they can do is just 'act white'. Those are the dead ones and they start to die, as soon as they start hearing about making something of themselves."

"You know interviewer, no one can make something of himself. That is a fact. Trust me! They die young in our eyes. You also know Mr. Interviewer, parents, grandparents too, start telling them stuff and those fools listen to them. I was told all that and I didn't listen to a word of it for it wasn't cool. It wasn't cool for my brothers and not the group I started hanging with when I was four."

"You see Mr. Interviewer my home is on and in the streets. I remember running on the streets late at night and my mother jumped all over my act; but that was before the streets gave me an act to have and live. My mother didn't know any better and I had to go out and prove to her I was a man when I was seven. So you see me today. I am a man! Patience Mr. Interviewer I am coming to an end, so we can part ways as friends."

"We young Black men die young because we are suppose to and that is the fate of those who so chose to do so. Some die like soldiers and others are simply targets. Don't ask me if it is right or wrong? There are no right's nor wrong's in the world around here. It's just what is happening today that counts and there is no tomorrow. That is why it is so easy to die young. If you think about tomorrow you are dead. I don't want to be tomorrow, I want to be today, right now, not later! Young is today, tomorrow is old and already dead."

"Mr. Interviewer please think about these words:

We insiders are born to die for the amusement of others. We are one of life's entertainments and I am an optimist."

"Remember my friend:
When you die you die from life and you die from memory."

"The 'Gap' you keep referring to is the place, where we go to be forgotten. The 'Gap' is where the unemployable and unwanted go to be forgotten. It is a safe haven from being responsible for yourself."

Interviewer's after thoughts and analysis

I never saw Tyronne again. I came away from the interview with mixed emotions.

I thought many times about the limits he placed on himself and how he let the world, that world immediately around him, dictate what his life would become. It seemed to define his possibilities and he never challenged those limitations. Despite the apparent fact that there were others in his life, who wanted him to go beyond his current and probable future, he didn't hear them.

But we are talking about the use of reason with a young man, whose understanding of reason was partial and woefully inadequate for a future in adulthood. His greater sense of security was definitely tied to his identity with his real and imagined entourage.

I can now understand why so many young Black men, and others, die so young on the streets. But I found it curious how he twisted from my perspective, the concept of death on the street. But again, was it really twisted?

Insights

The interview, in fact this particular interview, opened up a new way of thinking for "Mr. Interviewer." He shared with me what I now call the Tyronne Theater of Complex Context. Like a play in a theater, context is alive and shifts about without rules. I see something happening within his theater. Let me indulge your imagination with a few thoughts.

Think about an ancient Japanese Kabuki play. In those plays you are pressed into seeing many plays in one. The roles of the players take on deep meanings, which require forced concentration to understand what transpires during the overlapping scenes.

The actors learn their skills and artistry through understudying with family members. Therefore, each player learns from generations before in how to "live" on the stage. They learn layers upon layers of actions, protocols, expressions of feelings and the making of sounds for all to hear. Each actor is a personalized, living craft.

Ty's interpretation of street life taught him some of the roles of the street. Each passed down from one generation to another on the overlapping stages of neighborhoods. Similar to Kabuki, the audience in the neighborhood recognizes the roles being played, by the masks worn by the players on the streets. Even their styles in movement are historical.

What should I make of his assertion that to go to school and go on with an ascending life is death? Perhaps, it means you die in the eyes of the street. Maybe you die because you failed living to the codes of the entourage scene.

Granted there are those who do die, physically, and usually due to an act of violence. In my opinion, **the engine supporting the "Gap" is found in his assertions: going on with your life can lead to death and no one listens to him. So why should he listen to them, let alone find actionable value in what they have to say?**

Are we dealing with a viewpoint where the gap represents a symbol or symptom of death? If we are going to deal with the Perfect Black Man, does he die, that is to say, does his identity die, when he must compete in a world where he doesn't believe he can win? Losing is a big thing in Ty's interpretation of life. But, what is winning in his life, what does winning look like to him and what happens when he does win?

Who cares if he does or doesn't win, especially at life? I think he could talk endlessly about failing, but would clam-up when talking about succeeding.

Like fatalism, failure is a resource for feeding the souls of the lost? If so, are we teaching, through myopic expectations, young Black men to embrace failing, out of fear they will succeed?

My final thoughts: On young Black men

a. Young Black men live in inadequate places with inadequate educations. Inadequate educations are inherently inadequate for creating successful lives. Many public school districts and some private schools, create illusions of providing adequate educations. Too many educators use illusions to teach and grade student progress. Then what is represented by the term, "an adequate education?" I believe an adequate education is inadequate for students, because it works along a teacher controlled regression line, inherently skewed downwards for certain students.
b. Young Black men have few options in expecting to see tomorrow;
c. They prefer to not live in the outside world, instead live risks to the max. lives, navigating in the dark, along a constant edge of self-destruction;
d. My biases come out here, again, as I wonder about young Black men, who can find no comfort in gaining knowledge about the earth, especially outside their world called the street and the neighborhood.

e. For them as for many of their role models, ignorance is life's way in teaching you about yourself. It is secure and never questioning, never demanding. Ignorance is like a faithful, affection starved pet, that provides unconditional love in return for a little attention.

I am glad I was able to "pass" in his eyes. The interviewer.

The Pit School

In the pit: "If we all be smart, then none of us can be smart!"

The three boys ran as quickly as they could into the woods. Their goal, a favorite hiding place—The Pit School. Bill had the prize they had waited weeks to see, it was neatly wrapped and it was like gold to them.

Looking back to see if anyone had paid attention to their scurrying around, they took their usual route into the pathless woods. It was late in the afternoon and they wouldn't be missed for a couple hours. Finally, they stole into the brush pile.

As Billy was the first to enter, he was immediately startled to see, in front of him, his older brother sleeping away. Stretched out with the blanket from their family's only bed, John-Hunter was not in a mood to be awaken by anyone, let alone this threesome. But it was too late, the other two rushed through the opening and made enough noise that John-Hunter sat up, most displeased with the sudden interruption.

John-Hunter was unaware that the three younger members of the farm had made the little hideaway their Pit School. He saw the package in Billy's hands and reached for it. But Billy pulled back before John-Hunter could wrestle it free.

An argument began over why he was there and why they were there as well? John-Hunter was starting to awaken and wanted to know what was in the package?

Finally, and reluctantly, Bill told him it was a book. John-Hunter's eyes widened against his nose to his ears. A book was against the law for them to even hold. It was against the law for them to learn how to read. He wanted to beat his brother and the others, but knew he would later have to explain his action to his parents. Instead he insisted on seeing the book.

Billy handed it over, still wrapped. John-Hunter had never handled a book before. He was fifteen and had only seen two books in his life—A Bible and a children's tale. But he couldn't read, so it was of little matter of what he was now holding.

He told the boys they would have to return it the house and never mention it again to anyone. But Billy knew they couldn't, for their friend had given it to them. They could and would never say who was the friend. Then John-Hunter said he would hide it from them and they could not have it back.

Billy wanted to fight his brother, but knew it was impossible, for he was only eight and too small to beat his bigger brother senseless. He was also wise enough to know combat was not a good idea. Someone could get hurt.

The threesome began panicking and feeling a little like crying. Finally, John-Hunter looked at them and asked a question passed down from generation to generation: "What makes you think you can be smart?"

He finished his tirade with a point that hit the small boys like a two-by- four: "Don't you know that if all of us can't be smart, then none of us can be smart! So why are you trying to act White, you simpletons can't read. Reading is something that only White people can do. And you ain't White!"
From that day forward his little Pit School closed forever, but some years down the road, it was given a proper burial.

A few decades into the future, Billy wrote about his recollection of that moment. He called it: **"The Lamentation for Fools."**

The Report: Guest Op-Ed, Sometime, Somewhere

The speaker made his presentation to the committee. Behind the presenter, a local consultant, who knew his subject well, sat along with a throng of locals who also knew the subject, but from a host of other perspectives.

The Chair of the committee thanked the speaker for his efforts. Placing the report on the table he immediately condemned the report, just shy of tearing it up in public view.

Obviously, taken aback by the sudden and unanticipated attach, the presenter demanded an explanation for the negative response from the Chair. His attacker looked at him, rolled his eyes, but knew others where watching him closely; so he sat back and waited for the right time to speak.

A long ten seconds later he finally spoke. He looked down at the report and quietly, turned it over—face down; a gesture with some hidden purpose from this observer's position. Slyly he looked up a the presenter and simply said, "Its just another report and we have read all of this before."

"Amen brother!" yelled a voice about five rows deep in to the over crowed audience. A chorus of others chimed in with agreement. But, what were they agreeing with?

The report, as presented that night, simply stated that the structure of the agency would have to change to really address the needs of the community it was suppose to serve. But the document included some points few people apparently did not want to hear.

For instance, it was stated that many of the recommendations had previously been made in earlier reports, over the past ten years . Consequently, the history trail of those reports left little trace of any effectiveness in their implementation. Consequently, the latest of the report's recommendations included some specific changes in approaches to resolving the agency's issues and other dilemmas.

The Chair, the committee members and others in the audience were aware of those issues and for good reason. Many of them had participated in the earlier attempts to implement the recs. of the aforementioned reports. It was thus noticed with some irony that some of the critics of the current report, where heavily vested in the failures of the earlier projects.

Exasperated, the presenter turned to members of his team for support. The support came in the form of a thirty-five year old lawyer, who had grown up in the community. Also, a twenty-five year old Ph.D. in psychology—but an outsider as well.
It should be emphasized that the lawyer, by the nature and extent of her education and economic standing, was also an outsider to the community; despite the fact her family had been in the neighborhood for over a hundred years. Which, by the way, was nearly five times as long as a majority of local residents' families.

The pair stood up and approached the podium. They looked at the Chair and then turned to the audience. Whereupon they asked three members, pulled at random, to come forward. The Chair asked if this were necessary and the Ph. D. turned and only answered emphatically, "Yes!"

Facing away from the committee the pair moved their three "volunteers" to three positions facing the mass of faces in the audience. The volunteers consisted of two men and one woman. Standing they appeared in a quandary as to what was expected of them?

But they stood motionless, waiting for further instructions.

The attorney walked to the back of the room. While the Ph. D. turned to the podium, facing the audience and positioned the woman volunteer just to his right. The two men were placed right and left of him.

Once the lawyer placed herself at the back of the room, she asked the woman next to the Ph.D. about the protest against those who killed the eight year old boy, during a drive-by shooting five years earlier and how the shooting was detailed in one of the earlier reports. (Although there were countless witnesses no one was arrested for the murder.)

The woman remembered the shooting, but for the life of her she recalled nothing of a protest of the shooting. "What did the agency do?" inquired the attorney. The Ph.D. pulled out a paper from a folder. He quoted an earlier report:

"The agency believes that there is a genuine and measurable lack of interest by a majority of community members, in protecting its citizens from random, wanton acts of life threatening violence."

The woman turned and stared at him, he handed her the paper. Apprehension and confusion were beginning to control the moment. The doorways with exit signs over them started to look inviting to many sitting, now less patiently. The Ph.D. stared at the woman and asked why people did not protest the death of an innocent boy? Then he turned to the Chair and asked him? Neither answered.

Waiting for her turn, the attorney asked the man, stage right about why it was so hard for the community to support the changes the earlier reports had recommended?

Why was it so hard to help stem the violence in the neighborhoods? Where were the people who could protect the community from those who could destroy it?"

The grossly obese, normally verbose, backslapping, borderline practicing jibe fanatic, shifted his weight from his left foot to his right. He leaned forward as he was buying some precious time to think. Finally, he composed himself and shot a glance to the Doc before looking around at the audience for answers. Not one answer could be found in their eyes. All were as puzzled as he by the line of questions coming from the pair of inquisitors.

So, he looked down and took a short step forward. He looked up and stared at the attorney once again, but for a shorter moment.

He was not on trial, but he was a prisoner held by silence, for an event long past. Now he became the cold hand of justice, serving a summons to memories of an injustice to the dead. Cornered and with no where to go, the pressure got to him and he started telling a story. It was a true recollection that was never meant for public consumption. His cell door opened.

"You see Miss the earlier reports, like the present one, ah, is it where or were right? Whatever! Yet they all had one major flaw. They assumed, like the people in the agency, that this community wants change. But, the flaw wit that flaw was and still is to this moment, that we want others to change, especially the agency. We do not want to change, you see what I mean?"

"Of course, please excuse my words if they are wrong, the paradox is that if the agency actually changed, the community would have to change in support.

It's the same for the schools, for the park board, for the city and all its departments."

His body language began to relax.

"So the game goes on and on and on!" he said. The speaker took a couple seconds to reflect upon what he had just admitted. Instead of looking at the audience, he now focused on the eyes of the lawyer standing in the middle of the back of the room.

"You see we cannot afford to change. We just cannot afford it! Others must change to help us including institutions, etc. You know, you must know????"

He was finished in more ways than one. He went on after a few seconds of composing himself.

"We are owed and because we are owed we dare not change. What happens to us if they do not owe us?" The back slapper, went silent. This was a most revealing question and moment in the life of the community, as it spoke volumes.

The other man, stage left, felt the game changing spirit and added, "Yes, the game is about who wins and who loses, isn't it? We want ours, but what do we want so badly that we are willing to sacrifice nothing? We want others to do everything for us. Yet, we are the ones who really lose with such an attitude."

Both inquisitors stood patiently. The Chair wanted to stop the inquiry, but for once he had enough sense to remain silent and let fate be placed in the hands of the outsiders.

The Doc looked around at the faces in front of him. He caught himself stopping a temptation to lecture them. Instead, he resorted to asking them to look at what they and the agency alone must accomplish to overcome the violence, visibly eroding life away in their streets and neighborhoods?

He returned to the theme of protests over the deaths of innocent people, innocent children, by random drive by shootings, especially at social events and into homes? Why do people watch drug deals going down and say nothing? Oh, but complain they will and perhaps most about police brutality. For the police, it is always a no-win situation, when trying to overcome crime in places living passively and indifferently with crime.

Yes, it was a passive crew that sat between he and the attorney. They listened but there were no Amen's, no nodding heads, just eyes counting their feet. The Doc looked at a dying corpse of a once thriving town. Each head in the room represented a nail in the coffin of the community. The town was dead, but only those in the cemetery were certain of that fact.

A social wasting disease had infected the hearts and minds of the people. Without question the pain from wasting away could no longer be hidden from sight. Any outsider could see the scarring effect on the social tissue in every face. Streams of tears had created washed out canyons of dreams. What was left were hollowed out lives. Such is the effect of denial and shameful disinterest in a collective tomorrow.

The Doc looked back at the attorney, then at the consultant. Together they said nothing else, but just walked out of the meeting. In the wake of their departing steps, they left a strong feeling of disgust over the eroding place called a community and the impotency of the agency.

The community was disappearing, despite the fact it didn't know it. Denial is not priceless. As the trio walked away, they heard a faint pounding of a hammer. It was over!

Chapter Three: Life in a far away land

When are you old enough to know better?

The cop listened to the call, a response to a 9-1-1. A neighbor spotted two young men brandishing, big black pistols. The young men were tall and too big to play with toy guns.

The neighbor told the dispatcher that other young men, congregating nearby, were quickly moving away from the pair. A second resident called in to confirm the scene. Three police cars were dispatched and converged upon the block from different directions.

Only one car, with two officers inside, appeared upon the street with the young men plainly in sight. There were no sirens. One of the young men saw the patrol car and started pointing his weapon towards the car. Then both of them started pointing at the others boys, who were still backing away.

The patrol car rolled quietly towards them and when they were about thirty yards away one officer go out. He walked to an alley way, where he linked up with the officers from one of the other dispatched units. Meanwhile, both neighbors kept relaying the actions of the two men to the dispatcher, which was also being recorded. Both young men or boys pulled out extra clips from their jackets.

Now the street was empty except for a couple passing cars, neither slowed down. The police motioned them on, while other units came upon the block and started blocking off the street on both ends. The traffic flow stopped.

The cops were now beginning to quietly approach the young men. No sirens, no bull horns or dogs.

There were five policemen, all of whom were of the same ethnic group as the gun holders. They began a cornering maneuver.

One squad car turned the corner from behind the boys. At that point one young man tried to hide his pistol under his shirt. While the other raised his weapon and pointed it at the car. The officer turned on his red lights and warned off the others, who were now closing in and witnessed the suspects actions firsthand.

The street was completely abandoned of cars. A few people watched, hiding their faces from the action in the scene nearby, but still watching nonetheless. The officer in the lead car got out without trying to startle the men-childs. He kept a hand on his holstered pistol, but remained behind the opened door of his vehicle. From there he closely watched the hands of both boys. One still held his pistol, but slightly, ever so slightly, pointed the barrel away from the patrolman. The other had his hand on his weapon, but it was hidden away under his shirt.

The lead officer started talking to them. They watched him and kept shifting their hands around their pistols. The one who had hidden his pistol had now removed it and began gangsta aiming towards the policeman. His firearm was still holstered.

The cop kept talking to both of them, distracting them as the other officers moved closer from their blind sides. Finally, the other officers made their presence known, closing off all escape routes.

The officer next to the car could hear the apparent leader of the pair, hissing as he urged his friend to hang with him. He was telling him to stay cool, and adding that they were going to be heroes like those cool people on TV. He was heard saying, "Brother, these cops can't touch us, for the community is with us!"

The other officers still had their pistols holstered. Suddenly the lead boy made a few steps towards the cop and the car, moving quickly and menacingly fast. As suddenly, he stopped, pivoted and swung the pistol chest high towards the other cops. They were standing next to a house owned by a neighbor. Under greater direct threat, the policemen and policewomen spread apart and pulled their pistols, but kept them pointed down.

The ground between the cops and the boys was now small and growing, ever deadly. The second boy started shaking his head, his eyes were widening with fear. His breathing was visibly deeper, while sweat was pouring off his chin. He lowered his gun and slowly backed away from his friend.

Gradually, he leaned down, not saying a word, while dropping his eyes to the gun held loosely in his hand. By this point he was standing behind his friend. He placed the gun on the ground, stood up and raised his hands. He put them behind his head and then placed himself down on the ground—arms wide out and stretched ahead.

His friend turned to see where he was. He saw the "traitor", lying on the ground. He aimed his pistol at his betrayer's head.

The police now aimed their weapons at the boy with the gun. He was standing, threatening loudly his intent to shoot his onetime partner. The officer in the car started moving his vehicle closer. The once upon a time young man turned, now somewhat startled by the change in events. Everything was speeding up. Everything was not happening the way it happens in the movies. The police were not afraid of him. Wasn't he the hero?

Outwardly, he looked defiant and sneering against the odds of his situation. Suddenly he laughed like a giggly baby, while trying to intimidate fate.

A childlike stand off of what was once eternity, was quickly replaced by the official business end of 9mm reality. The boy looked around to see what options he had available? None! None existed for escape. Even fewer chances for living remained in his mind. Not surprisingly, this boychild did not know how to make sense of a senseless situation. He was not accustomed to thinking for himself.

Fueled by fear and an odd sense of unfairness, he started yelling at the cops, who with cold faces just stared back, ignoring his taunting and boasting. In the meantime his friend had crawled to an officer and was now handcuffed, searched and removed away from the scene.

He abandoned his partner who was officially alone. All could see he was becoming more agitated and kept swinging around from cop to cop with his gun. Yes, he was alone, words he kept mumbling to himself. His mental state was deteriorating.

Some guy from a distant house, yelled out, "Shoot, shoot!" The police glanced angrily at the idiot. Suddenly, a fire cracker went off behind a house. The boy ducked. A news helicopter moved in for evening news shots. None of the officers moved an inch. They just continued watching as one talked to the isolated boy with a man's gun in his hand.

His earlier audience had all tired of the spectacle. They could watch the climax later on the news. In truth, there was nothing new to be called news for them.

Finally the patience of the cops was starting to wear thin. But they stood still and just kept talking with him. A police supervisor arrived on the scene and watched from afar. The situation was hopeless for the boy. What does a young Black man, still thinking a child's game, do with what little hope he has had for life as it vanishes?

He couldn't wake up. He was awake! He just didn't know it.

He turned the gun towards his head and closed his eyes. It was too late for the cops to say anymore. The neighbors hung up their phones connected to the dispatcher.
Later that evening: "And this just in from our eye witness reporter......"

The news reported the death of a boychild. It reported nothing about his life. High quality journalism at its well awarded best. Please Paddy Chayefsky, come back and write a different ending to your story. Help the news save us from the news and ourselves.

Holding Back Tomorrow

If you like to think about "lessons learned," then this paper is just right for you to read.

When a culture decides to hold back tomorrow, it does so with many interesting mechanisms. It applies ignorance as if it were intelligence and looks at itself, satisfied with its own greatness. Once a community or culture can achieve holding back tomorrow, there is no tomorrow. In another way, it can hold back the future by resurrecting a so-called "ideal" from its past.

This process requires creating a lot of myths about its own history. Of course, myths also create casualties and the first is the Truth. The Truth is sculpted in the hardest stones compressed from inalterable facts. The second is memory. Repression is the designated slayer of memories and group-think is collectively called "our hangman."

The innocent must be reminded that myths are self-serving mental beasts. They evolve to justify the existence of "classified" traditions, held secret beyond collective memories. Now, I'd like to explore one of those myths with you.

When a culture looks inward and seeks to hide the wealth of its memories, it runs a risk. If it pursues this course, it can assume no responsibility for any consequences. In reality, by ignoring the future and the outside, it cannot honestly blame anything except itself. Yet, this is a path many groups are taking in America today. Where a calamity awaits in the form of another economic catastrophe.

We have witnessed a sample of that calamity: i.e. our current style of recession. Let me explain.

I will start with an examination of what has happened to us.

Then I will move to what will happen in the not too distant future. It begins with a simple observation of who should live where and why and why not?

When America began its gradual post WWII migration into suburban living, it established a social brand of small communities on the edges of urban cores. With this design came an assumption: only like-minded people, culturally and ethnically identical, could and would exist side-by-side. It also assumed that our society would respect and sanction this arrangement forever.

More importantly, all of this was predicated upon a belief that incomes would rise to support larger and larger homes as well.

Larger homes grew and grew. Not surprisingly, their costs and interest rates grew in tandem: all in defiance of gravity. We too often forget, human egos are not bound by gravity. What a pity!

People believed growth was eternal like the sun. America's Icarus Complex always tries to fly high

It happened, but not beyond a few decades. What transpired was that gravity trumped assumptions made by men and women about their collective futures. Yes, it is true, women and men do not have control over the future.

In America our memories, be what they may, are becoming addicted to forgetting our own history. It seems that history has become something adverse to the American psyche. Especially, when our memories are confronted and tested against new information from current events. It is odd, but it appears new dis-information conveniently overrides, if not erases older, definitive records, usually called facts. It is interesting how those who should remember and know the facts, somehow catch a fever of amnesia.

It is actually critical for us to remember that the lessons from the Depression were never taken for granted. Eventually, they eroded as older family members disappeared into eldercare facilities. This was all part of the encroachment of modern times, but nothing is safe in modern times—not even modernity. What has happened in our modern communities? Let's return to the houses that make up those fail-safe neighborhoods.

Like the communities, homes grew in size as well. With the expanding sizes came an incentive to keep buying larger houses, to match growth in personal impression building and a hyper self-inflating sense of worth. Suddenly, an illusion began feeding on itself.

The Trap

A trap was set by reality and its ally, gravity. Suddenly to "everyone's" surprise gravity received its order to spring the trap. Down came the value of homes, sinking many with unloadable debt.

It was quick, exceedingly painless at first, then pain rose to deadly proportions. Shock and awe stalked the surprised. The personal catastrophes spanned social economic spheres from high and mighty to the lowest schmucks on the American landscape. In many once hyper-promoted developments, quick drive by's now reveal natural disaster proportions of constructed wastelands.

Efficiently erected communities were turned from landmark status symbols, into decapitating slaughterhouses for headlined economic sectors. Money pits grew into open pit quarries—lifetimes wide.

The immutable lifeblood of the economy, DEBT, thoroughly coagulated in the hardening veins and arteries of financial and commercial institutions.

Dollarquakes and accompanying stockshocks are still being felt, years after the first signs of tremors under the foundations of the money world. It was another, "This can't be happening!" moment. Except we were there!

Tomorrow

America spends trillions of dollars on its physical security. We invest comparatively pennies on securing its emotional security, for present and future generations. So, may I ask who is going to live in those larger than life homes, situated in larger than life neighborhoods built to secure myths?

Again, for the uninformed in the audience, history has the same question, as it begets lessons to inform the future. Will anyone remember to recall the lessons? Or will 2006 play it again?

What happened? One day millions of people awoke to find out they no longer had jobs, their invested wealth had disappeared and their dreams were lost beyond memory. All of this has produced a startling fact: today not enough people have the wealth and sustainable means to live in pre-2008 lifestyles.

The Baby-boom bubble has gone bust; with it much more has fallen away than millions have wanted to imagine. But not all was lost.

Debt created another bubble for us to live in for a long time to come. Except this one is more like bust-proof.

The Baby-boom was born from the deprivations of the Depression and the pre-fears and post-glories of WWII. Yes, America can lay claim to many feats of success during and after the war; but it forgot to not make history angry through all of its constant boasting. Americans, especially those who continually cry for a return to our fabled American dream, never learned that history does not share certainty with any human, who dictates his claim to power. That is an act of corruption. Such acts are never immutable.

History knows how power can corrupt, and it can corrupt absolutely. But, history also has a depth of integrity, which goes beyond those of saints.

History gives moderated control to those who are willing to create a positive, new tomorrow. It does this especially for men and women, who are genuine in creating benefits for all and not for the sole benefit of a privileged few. But history is not blind and all trusting.

A regulating eye constantly watches human talents, to spot players in games known for self-destruction. Powerful people and their institutions are extremely capable of destroying themselves. Unfortunately, they take the innocent along with them in their falls. And fall they will—as they work hard and invest heavily to make it their destinies. Death, advanced by senility and products of incalculable vanities, wait patiently for them.

The American Dream

For instance, in my opinion, the heart of our fabled American Dream of the 20's thru the 70's stopped, post Viet Nam war. It died between the 70's thru 1995 (est.). Even the word "fascinating" does not do justice in capturing how **TIME,** itself, did not move slowly enough, for many to register its passing.

Ultimately the Dream, even as a mirage, could no longer stand for anyone forgetting its role in American economic history. It campaigned for a second life. In 2009 it appointed thousands of disciples to relight its name from sea to shining sea. Nonetheless, it still struggles to regain its place in the hearts and minds of the multitudes. Like Time, the world has moved on. The American Dream didn't!

It had fallen unconditionally in love with itself. It did this while admiring its own out-dated images. They were reflected in a broken mirror lying on the floor, forever missing millions upon millions of discarded pieces.

It is 2011 and the multitudes have been re-educated by the greatest teachers of all: DIRECT, PAINFUL AND LIFE CHANGING EXPERIENCES. They see a myopic American Dream of old, vainly conscripting the past in trying to hold back their tomorrows.

Visible to all, there is a paradox when trying to hold back tomorrow. If others continue trying to lay claim to their own dreams, then the American Dream will protectively fold inward. Collapsing! Eventually suffocating all it can reach, while rotting ideas and silently creating an implosion of innocent souls.

To reiterate: The old American dream is rotting away. Rightfully so, new generations have begun inventing impressive, far more holistic dreams. Their tomorrows exist outside of self-limiting and manufactured schemes; where one-size-fits-all types of thinking.   The new dreams will adapt to their own realities and not cross-over to those of their parents' or grandparents' generations.

A Key Lesson To Remember

No country can progress by seeking refuge in its past. Therefore, any and every country, through divesting itself from its future; makes its people refugees in their own homes. And there the feeble, the foolish and fact-adverse will have no choice but to await for the return of or passing of TIME.

The days of the Baby-boomers are fleeting. Yes, we have to start making way for new ideas, most from younger people. They need places and spaces, from which they can earn their time in the sun.   Consequently, my demographic cohort's departure represents a needed opportunity for our next generations' dreams to flourish.

They know, better than we, their tomorrows' must be earned and disentangled from America's economic debris of the 1980's thru 2011. I hope we have the guts and good sense to get out of their way, and only provide advise upon request. I also hope they have the guts, a sense of history and good sense to know when to ask for advise.

It is a dream: but may we all work diligently and unselfishly, to create the best America imaginable. We can support the improvement in living standards for all the people in the world, and not for just a few.

The Great American Transitions

Thinking of debris, the Baby-boomers must accept a silent challenge to clean up, as much as possible, the junk blocking the doorways of the future. We can call the doorways: The Great American Transitions.

I offer two pieces of thought:

First, we must identify as many half-truths and points of dis-information, currently floating around on the Internet and airways. We need to instill a cultural discipline of expecting people to incorporate only real facts into news reports, business and political discourses.

Soft, Semi-transparent Fraud is costing America its self-respect and the respect of the rest of the world; plus an inestimable amount of money. In addition, we must require schools to help students learn how to carry on dialogues with other people, in face-to-face encounters and not simply through texting.

Next to water, air and food, Communication is the key substance of life in a democracy and capitalistic society. It also means, we must face up to some real truths, many want to ignore or try to let die through neglect.

The act of retaining painful Truths about America is a steep and necessary price to pay, for creative transformation into a New America. We must also set ourselves free from media and politically driven vain glorious myths, which solely benefit the vain glorious in our society.

Second, we must accept that we are no longer the center of the world. America is not an Empire, despite the best efforts of a few to make it a modern day Rome. Fortunately, they failed and the tools used by them for their failure were the same tools used by Empire builders throughout the history of the world. The rest of us suffered from their detachment with reality and history. Vanity costs!

The World's Calendar

America's evolving generations are confronting a new earth, which will live by a World Calendar and not an American-centric calendar. What this calendar will look like remains to be seen, but it is already living in our times. What is forthcoming?

America will share shelf space with other cultures in the markets of dreams.

Americans will finally come to recognize we are not alone in the Universe.

Chapter Four: Club Schadenfreude

- **Date and place: You be the judge, for it happened not too long ago, near you, very near you indeed!**

An imaginary presentation? Perhaps, perhaps not!

Good morning. I hope you don't mind the absence of computer aided graphics for my talk? They get in the way of stories.

I appreciate your organization allowing me to meet with you this morning. It is a pleasant, even a gratuitous timing to talk with you. Especially on the topic that I will share on this very nice Spring day.

You are the perfect group of professionals to hear this presentation. I believe there are judges, teachers, bankers, politicians, accountants, CEO's, non-profit executives, welcome all and thank you for coming.

The topic is about something that I've come across and it is an idea, I think needs to be talked about in light of our country's eroding economic climate. I will couch it in the form of a legacy: a metaphor or maybe another term, but it's something I think needs to be discussed. So before it is presented, I would like to share a story for you to think about, over the next few hours and days. It begins this way.

A few years ago I spent a little time in a California community and it had a large downtown business district. One night after dinner I walked along a street in the district and came across an odd site. The air temperature was not hot, but comfortable. I had a light jacket on or I had on a light jacket (excuse me.)

As I walked along I saw a "gentleman" sitting on a pile of cardboard, with his back to a wall. He had ten, old canvas bags stashed neatly around him. This was a modern, model street bum.

He looked pretty shabby, wearing an assortment of mismatched threads for clothes. At least he had some shoes. Obviously, he was not an advocate of socially appropriate attire. That was not a big issue for him.

But in front of him and on top of another sizable piece of cardboard was what at first appeared as a roll of carpet. Instead, it turned out to be a rolled up piece of leather. And what was he doing with the leather? He was drawing something on its stained, oak colored, smooth side.   From a distance it looked like several scenes, with multiple horizontal lines scratched across its width.

Moving in closer, I finally saw that he was drawing images, from about the knee down, of people's legs. The scene depicted single legs as they walked pass. Amazingly, they were all of one leg per person. Out of an inherited passion to play the role of a grand inquisitor, I lowered myself down and dropped some money in a little collection box, already full of one dollar bills. My God, I spotted a hundred dollar bill! He said thank you.

So I asked if I could share the spotlight with him for a few minutes? He said of course and he moved over and gave me a little spot on his paperboard. It was his way of moving over on a couch, except he was sharing his few square feet of cold concrete. I pressed my back against one of his bags. He said it was another friend's bag, his only earthly possessions. He was its caretaker for the evening.

Apparently, the group of people, like himself, look after one another. I thought to myself, how amazing! Who would have thought any down and outers, would trust another down and outer with their worldly possessions?

I became really intrigued! Could they actually trust one another and do they have a code of ethics? Eventually, people started walking past and occasionally someone deposited something and again he said thank you. Despite the way I looked, I soon got the impression that people thought I was also begging. In fact I had on a new leather jacket, nice pants, plus polished shoes. I didn't fit the image except for one thing: both the bum and I were Black.

He seemed comfortable and surprisingly content, as people walked by our temporary occupied spot on the cold earth. As I am compelled, I asked him about his life story and he told me, openly and without a hint of warranted shame.

The Bum's Story Line

In summary, his life was a mix of growing up in the Midwest, with a few years spent in the military (combat included with wounds from head to feet.) When he was delivered back into civilian life, he had a decent job. An uncontrolled indulgence in drug cocktails, helped him spend his life rotting downhill.

He admitted combat can do that to you. The bullets didn't take him out, but life after war made him an easy target, and the drugs hit their mark every time. He still bleeds from the pharmaceuticals. Pop and Bliss!

Eventually, with nowhere else to run, he found himself on the street (our American lifestyle for a last resort.) At that point, I couldn't help myself, so I asked him about his artwork.

He just pointed to it and then I saw he had written a title on the top. It read, *"You be the judge."*

We continued talking about a number of topics. After sitting there for an hour, it became apparent that he was talented in not only art, but also in understanding people, especially human nature. He was not a lightweight, so to speak. His language was very "deep," even thoughtful despite his circumstances. He was living his chosen life style. It was a lifestyle most people would not want for themselves or anyone else, except for a few in-laws perhaps.

And it dawned on me. I really wanted to buy that piece of artwork from him. In my mind the image of lines of legs and shoes, stockings, dresses, Italian made coats, basketball shoes, of sockless legs, you name it, they all went by one leg at a time. The bum had them moving in different directions: right to left and left to right. As we sat there, he started telling me that this was a legacy piece for him. It represented his life.

For some reason, perhaps fed by his patience with me, I felt emboldened to ask a few, more personal questions. He wasn't going anywhere and I wasn't going away. But first I wanted to incite a little reflection on his part.

My questions had to reach a higher bar. He knew more than I on some features of life. I was now all ears and he helped me unlock my significantly closed mind.

My first question focused on the story behind the images of the legs?

He explained he was trying to depict the world from his level of view. Sitting on concrete can give you a unique perspective on life, you see. He only looked up at a few faces upon request. Expressed more pointedly, my bum said he was looking from the knees down.

That range of body space let him study and understand people from his level, in his space. The bum didn't need to see their faces, nor upper body language. His chosen perspective mimicked what a small child would see if walking among giants: adults. I was going to ask him about the sound of their footsteps, when....

Suddenly, some money was dropped in "our" box. I looked up at two neatly dressed men. They were looking at me. It was obvious they recognized something was wrong with the contrasts in the picture sitting on the ground. I jumped up and reached out my hand and they shook it. Both spoke slowly, in slightly French/English flavored dialects.

As it turned out they were both from a French speaking country and were scientists. Not surprisingly, both were in town for a medical products convention. As we talked they admitted recognizing that I didn't belong in that situation and I told them they were right. But I explained that I was curious to talk to this gentleman and he offered to let me join him. Surprisingly, but not too much upon reflection, both asked to join us. Scientists, of course! The scene was becoming surreal.

So we sat, our out of place foursome, and chatted for a bit about life and about their work as scientists from a different world. No one else stopped to join us. As new-bees to the perspective, we watched as people casually walked by; many without looking down at us or stopping to place a little money inside the box.

At first I wanted the "bum" to vocalize his take on the situation. But, I was foolish to think so. Eventually, I found myself reflecting on the situation. Now, with the presence of the Ph.D.'s, I had much more to ponder.

Looking back from the safe distance of a few years, one thing I wish some of the other people had joined our unusual quartet. It would have been fascinating for them to have watched the spectacle of people walking by; but also in helping them create a new reference point in understanding the lives of people.

The bum did this -- day in and day out. It would take a few more days for me to fully appreciate, if ever, what he was doing. For instance, you looked up and watched the eyes. Many avoided contact with mine. I truly wanted to search inside their minds and see what they were thinking about us, down below. I presumed they were acutely aware we were outsiders to their worlds. Presumptions, presumptions, presumptions!

Eventually, the scientists, those Ph.D. fellas, left us to enjoy the cool breeze at ground level.

So, let's get back to the drawing.

My new friend used the interruption to masterfully reverse the interview. He asked me what I saw in his drawing?

I thought for a moment and it was easy to see that the drawing was about people and their movements in the world. Given the question, I leaned forward to look at it more closely. I started paying attention to the piece of people moving pass - past. In the drawing there is (excuse me again), there was no sense of movement. A pattern, a pattern, a pattern, yes there was a pattern.

It was near midnight and some of the people slowed down as they approached us. Others moved faster trying to escape the scene. I felt like they were walking pass real fast, so they could avoid a local street morgue of human road kill. And then it hit me: the title,
You be the judge.
You be the judge is about the people walking pass - past.

He wanted them to be the judges of his existence and in a way their own as well. Was he a judge? Yes, I concluded, he was a judge as well. Did he (their past) not let them pass, undisturbed, by his judgment of them?

At this point I want to introduce you to a wonderful opportunity. I have been going around the country, asking people to start chapters in a very enterprising organization I have named:

Club Schadenfreude.

I can tell that for many in the audience you are asking, "schada what?"

Schadenfreude is a German term, which means, quite simply: To find pleasure or joy in the misery or pain of others. It is an ancient concept, probably as old as human existence. Yet, I thought it needed some official representation in the world—an organization of merit. And what better way to give it some well deserved notoriety than by making it a club!

This club cost nothing to join, except you have to pledge to commit to applying yourself to one act of Schadenfreude every day. It can be accomplished at work, while driving, with your spouse, while playing with your children, walking along a street or even while worshiping at home, in your Church, your Synagogue or your Mosque (Blessed be to Allah.) The opportunities have no known human boundaries. But, I forgot one little catch to being a member.

You will have to enlist one true member per week. You must witness their act of Schadenfreude. They don't have to know you are watching. It is that easy. Yes, that is all and once you join you become a member for life. It is that simple. There are no forms to fill, no interviews, no pledges, just your word is needed that you will work hard to make the Club the largest in the world.

Imagine my friends, what it would be like to belong to the largest club in the world? For a moment, think of the economic benefits you would gain from associating with other members of such an illustrious crowd.

I let the audience absorb that point, while I watched their faces, most of which dared not look at me. Some knew I was staring right through them, to the depths of their exposed and barren souls.

So I took a deep gulp of air and looked to the back of the group, then to the sides. This took a few seconds. I wanted to ignite some tension in the room and let it build like a fire. It was now time to break the silence with an observation for local consumption.

I suggested that what I saw in the bum's drawing was his legacy. I saw the features of a club   He watched a spectacle every day and night as it marched past him. Perhaps spectacle is too strong a description; how about a parade of vanities, fears, joys, dreams, side shows, and on and on and on. What else?

Of course, every club must have a charter, but in this case each chapter must create its own. I explained to the group that I wanted to borrow a couple more minutes of their time. It was granted, but with some noticeable discomfort among a few, with eyes on their watches.

I asked them to think about the world passing by and about people who are different from our selves? How would we place them in the scheme of our lives and where do we place ourselves in the schemes of their lives? For instance, if we look down on others, we must ask who's looking down on us as they pass us in life? But more importantly, what do we feel about ourselves when people look at us?

I sat down on the edge of the stage and put my back to the podium. Then, I reached down on the floor before me and pulled up some card board to sit on. Leaning back and reaching behind the podium, I pulled out a rolled piece of leather with a bunch of drawings of legs.

Many people have asked to buy my legacy piece of art. But it is my legacy.   They will have to create their own.

Oh this is a heavy talk, but I wanted you to think about your membership in Club Schadenfreude. And when you donate money or when you see people and they're having hard times, as in this economy, what do you do?
Do you hire others to do that work for you?

When you finally see them, does the experience give you an "upper feeling", suggesting you're are actually smarter than them and that they are dumber than you? Are you becoming addicted to believing they deserve their pain and they deserve their misery and you have no need to be around them and they have no rights to be near you, even see you?

Is our country's prolonged economic drift, creating a class of untouchables, unseeables and immediately forgetables?

I'm feeling this too and it is contagious. It knows no colors, for it knows no social boundaries. Remember: the club only seeks and easily finds new members every day. Truly! New members fall over one another to join and rejoin every day. Thank you and don't forget:

You Be The Judge!

I walked to the back of the room and placed a small, extremely worn box on the table near the door.

Another letter and paper

Date: March 12, 2025
To: Dr. J.T. Kobayashi
        Professor Emeritus
From: Former Student
Subject: Attached—a short excerpt from a paper I wrote several years ago, January 5, 2011
        My question: What has changed?

Title: Club Schadenfreude and the world of the Perfect Black Man
Prologue on a human behavior known as Schadenfreude

A simple definition would go like the following: Observing with joy or pleasure or even excitement, the pain or suffering of someone. I will add that it can include watching not just an individual, but a large class of people, who may be deemed socially undesirable (for instance the financially or socially poor.) They must be poorer than you see yourself. In many respects this requires that the subject of Schadenfreude must be willing to cooperate .

As found in other instances, members of the Club can belong to other clubs, which are established to help those held captive (voluntarily or involuntarily) by the Codes of Behaviors of Schadenfreude.

Community based Munchausen,
aka Club Schadenfreude

In theory, it is possible that a person could watch, with glee, someone suffering from circumstances he or she did not create or even wish to maintain. An individual could resist applying personal energies to reduce or eliminate the personal pain of their suffering. Ironically, in many but not all situations, they have learned to wait for assistance from others. This waiting is justified when circumstances warrant. For instance, an elderly individual or a born child is abandoned or abused by adults. In those and many other situations the person, regardless of age, is comparatively helpless.

We would hope that genuine compassion would arise in the hearts, minds and souls of those, who profess to care about their fellow human beings. Sometimes, yes sometimes, those souls make space for compassion. For others, compassion is an actionable responsibility, left for seasonal offerings at church or at the office. Accountability? No!

The appearances of compassion are dependent upon money from outside the boundaries of the streets and families. But, the issues, which create the need for Schadenfreude are not dependent upon money as much as self-regulated human interaction.

Good Doctor: I had to stop here. I couldn't write about his anymore.

An addendum written a few months later:
Topics for future discussions:
"Shock and Awe"
Faux compassion
Anti-abortionists, abortionists and children on the streets (where have all the saviors gone?)
"Those who can't – are left to teach!
Looking down on others
Forcing people to beg for donations, like bums on streets, pleading for mercy, forgiveness and the starving little boy in China, praying for change, reverse image today.

PETS

(Seriously Confidential, Please share only with trusted individuals)

During a conversation with a friend of a different ethnic persuasion from mine, we some how got into a discussion on ethnicity in America. For whatever reason he opened up to me and disclosed that many of his friends looked at a class of African Americans as "PETS." This is a more generalized term from which an urban variant is derived: "porch monkeys."

The feelings behind these types of terms are found all over the world and probably in every culture. So, let's just focus on one: PETS as applied in America and in reference to a class of people inside African-American communities.

Pets are a selected set of American men, women and children born of African-American dissent. Like animal pets, human pets need owners and the need for owners to have pets to care for and be begrudgingly loved by or at least feel a fantasized affection. Pet owners need pets and it is presumed, pets need pet owners. Some pets need and have pets too.

Not all people of American African-American descent are pets. To become a human Pet you must have a very low self-esteem. What that means: a person cannot have a strong belief in his value to others or to the world, not even to himself.

The attainment of this personal status begins in a home environment, where the child is not valued, despite a claim of loving the boy or girl. Often the child is viewed as an object of some sort. In some respects, the beginning of pet status can begin in a home.

Families with <u>Children As Objects</u> (CAO's) are found in every economic, social, ethnic and political group within America.

If not corrected in the home, the effects are transferred to other settings, like pre-school or later. The impact of this behavior easily guides a child's search for a place, where he is valued by others. If the immediate environment, including school, provides few if any options to be valued, then the child will find the satisfaction of that need in other settings.

Enter gangs, other family members, friends, life on the streets, police, jail, and an entourage of social service agencies.

Gangs and street life absolutely need new members, many of which become Pets of older members. This arrangement is a perfect setup for how the Pets will live throughout much of the rest of their adolescent and young adult lives. Given the possibility many will experience the juvenile and adult justice systems.

Thousands will eventually become Pets within those legal settings. A discussion on that topic must be "differed" to another day.

But, the process of becoming a Pet is reflected in how someone becomes indentured to the legal system for a specified amount of time.

As for Pets entering the radar of social service agencies, we have to run a quick overview of one example in the social service industry.

A popularized example of Pets in the making is found "When children want to have children." This is my take on a perennial situation in many communities (regardless of economic or social settings). Consequently, please bear with me for a few sentences of openly, non-romanticized thoughts.

When young women (as young as 12 or 13) want to have children, they become Pets, not unusually of older, but still, young men. In turn, their new born children become Pets as well. Unless, and it is a big unless, a young woman's extended family steps in to try and disconnect the baby from a cyclical, life-limiting Pet experience. So, I can change the description by calling it, "When Pets want to have Pets."

This example can be extended further to where you see houses occupied by several, non-coupled mothers, caring for young children. The fathers probably don't support the mothers nor the children; but they may occupy a significant amount of time with the women. Now, consider all of the above as background information.

From here we add a strong depth of context to ground Pets, into our American economic-political-social psyche, via a set of cyclical schemes.

Observe: this is neither a "Red State" nor "Blue State" thing." Nor is it captive to a conservative vs liberal field exercise. It is simply an American thing, not dominated by any political, economic and social persuasions. Again, it is color blind. Let's look at Pets, in formal settings, but...--- first:

Yes, it is complex! Please don't look for any simple viewpoints, which lead to foolishly simple solutions.

What I ask is that you apply an honest, multi-sourced, deeply informed, fully vetted, fact-based and balanced critical viewpoint, with a touch of imagination in understanding Pets. Whether you provide any empathy or sympathy for them is left to your discretion.

Regardless of your social status, PETS are all around you.

Agency Affect[2]

As with myths about slaves in different societies, Pets love being pets -- so it is believed by some people. They occupy and meet a set of needs for the "owners." In the context of this essay, some of the owners are white and some are black. We can find Pets in their birth neighborhoods, churches, and peer groups. Inevitably, established and potential outside social service agencies vie for resources and sometimes, media attention to support Pets.

Let me clarify a key point. Pets come in all shapes, sizes, ethnicities, religions and agencies. They are typically poor, but not necessarily[3]. At times they are employed by agencies dedicated to help support Pets. When you cannot be an owner, the next best thing is to become a care provider of Pets. But with a little twist!

This is an opinion

A few care providers thrive on helping Pets, thus they become enablers and delay or prevent them from losing their status as Pets. *The story gets a little sticky here.* I am suggesting some people may emotionally enjoy a presumed need they feel from Pets; because they are Pets and need to be cared for by a given person. Why?

---

[2] Agency Affect includes social-emotional needs of public funding groups and institutional donors, whose bureaucracies are dependent upon the existence and logistical living needs of Pets. The Agency Affect requires competition among organizations for access to families or individuals deemed, voluntarily or involuntarily, in need of assistance. When a community is flooded with social service groups placed in block after block settings, then the Agency Affect goes into over-drive. When you add funding processes and annual budgetary practices, Agencies know they must provide numbers to demonstrate their efficacy as providers of services to target groups, including designated Pets. Pets can represent high value yields.

[3] Selective parts of the newslike/entertainment media own Pets. A few sports personalities are Pets. Some vain glorious politicians are bought and sold as Pets, by politically oriented influence media.

What if a person feels that Pets are incapable of taking care of themselves? Therefore, a calling can be found for a person's life through continually helping designated Pets. Consequently, Pets are enabled to remain Pets in a system, which incentivizes them to live off the system. I hope you are not surprised? Obviously, there are always incentives at play in this and other games. Nothing is free!

An aside: *(You can actually find examples of the Pet phenomena in business, government, military, non-profit and academic bureaucracies. Oops! That is a little secret, don't pass it on.)*

This arrangement is acceptable as long as the person is genuinely trying to help individuals remove themselves from the Pet rolls. But it is corrupted when an individual, even a professional, creates a way of keeping someone dependent upon the system. Of course, it also means that it becomes a reciprocating relationship as well. Think numbers, FTE's, bureaucracies and budgets.

What do Pets do for people?

Pets provide a need for an outpouring of compassion to take care of others. Enter the compassion industry, with hands held out for donations, and tax right offs waiting in the wings. The tax side is another industry altogether different and now under (temporary?) siege.

Financial imperatives are moving forward to besiege social and economic support systems. Now, after a variety of financial debacles and poor personal and cultural economic thinking, we are facing monumental shortages of funding at all levels of civil and family life. How cities, states and the patronage of the Federal government respond to these crises, will determine how the lives of ordinary people, like Pets, will trend through the next thirty years.

Benefits and Expectations: The Social Economics of Need[4]
Basic Image, circa 2010   Please read the footnote.

Let's take a young man about 12 years old. He has one sister and a single, unsupported mother (no paternal support**).   The young man has a price on his head, although he doesn't know it.** (Costs are best guess estimates.) We want you to build the numbers and see what you come up with, for what it cost a community to support the family and the young man, in particular, for a twelve year period.

Just jot down a few numbers. Don't worry, it is simply an exercise in envisioning reality. **Please add any cost areas, which have been omitted.**
Non-education community costs

Opportunity costs
> Family living costs

Educational expense from tax payer support:
>> Pre-school for two years
>> K-6 grade at $7,000 per year burden rate

Share of direct family support provided by governmental funds
> Child support
> Medical support
> Housing and transportation

Options:
>> Interaction with juvenile system for one year
>> Burden rate for service agencies

---

[4] America will not create an equal, nor fair system across the country to address the following situations and attending questions. We want to find pragmatic and viable answers: What is the minimum a community is willing to spend on the life of a child between the ages of birth and 12?

Criteria: a. Child will be given only an adequate education; b. He will not be expected to see the world beyond his immediate neighborhood; c. Community and family expectations are kept very low for his emotional and intellectual gains through his educational career. He is expected to drop out of school before his fifteenth year of age.

Non-governmental support
How many jobs are dependent upon the life of a child who is a
Pet

> Birth---pre-school
> K-6 education
> Without family separation experience
> With family separation experience

Please add your figures. What number did you derive from the
exercise?

$_____.00

Remember, we are only looking for a 12 year period. Imagine
his costs for a total of eighteen years. This would include a visit
or two with higher levels of the juvenile justice system. He has
extensive visitation rights in jails as well.

Non-profit's promotion
  We want YOU young man!

Service provider's mantra:
> **Follow the money that follows the child!**

Competition between agencies for access to the young man and
the financial value he represents to groups across social service
communities.

> Community support (not-for-profits) including religious
> institutions.
> Financial support dedicated to enhance a child's
opportunities
> to develop as a non-Pet participant.
> Camps
> After-school activities
> Tutorials services
> Public library related activities
> Community service activities
> Volunteer supported activities
> Police and community safety
> Food banks: participation in which programs
> Non-parks and recreation activities
> Big-Brother like agency support

* Now, reduce the number of children eligible for needing such

services; yet, the number of services made available will remain static, if not increase. What do you have happening in a community as a result?

* Or, increase the number of children and reduce the number of

services. The third possibility is to do both.

Adult Pet Maintenance Costs: For discussion purposes only

Overall, what do you estimate is the burden rate of one adult age, Perfect Black Man, for one year in an urban setting? (Without an incarceration experience.)
$ .00

What would a community save, including state supported institutions, if one hundred PBM's were taken off the PBM roll?
$ .00

If a PBM were to find and hold a full time job, at minimum wage in your state, how much money would he make in a year and how much taxes would he pay from his wages?
$ .00

How much money could a community save by converting a PBM from a non-wage earning member of society, into a wage earning and tax paying member of society?
$ .00

PET's will be revisited in Books Two and Three

Chapter Five: LifeBowl^{sm}: Session One

The Setting

_Life_Bowl^{sm(5)}: A privately sponsored, non-political, online competition, about life between two groups of young men. The young men are located in the offices of business development organizations, separated by both space and the digital age.

The faces of the participants are not shown. Only their hands are visible. Each young man is wearing a sweatshirt, which is the same type and color as worn by his team members. The members cannot wear rings or bracelets, nor show any insignia or tattoos. They are also asked to wear gloves to cover any other identifying marks. Their voices are masked to hide their identities.

As rewards for participating in the competition

Each participant receives stipends to support his current living situations.
Each competitor also receives purchase cards to a local grocery store.
Each young man receives library cards.

Each young man will receive a total of one hundred hours of free tutoring, across any of four academic/technical topics of choice. It is intended that they choose subjects, which can lead to helping develop pragmatic and useful work oriented skills.

---

[5] **_Life_Bowl^{sm}** continues in Soul Rot Book Two and Soul Rot Book Three.

The Moderator is an unknown, non-denominational, evangelical commentator. We hear only her voice. All questions are both read to the participants and displayed to them on monitors. Unless otherwise noted, they are given three minutes to respond, as a team, with their answers. The responses can be no longer than three minutes in length. Any use of profanity, signs, other vulgarities, street slang, or "you know" statements, will force an immediate disqualification of a team's response. There are no exceptions!

The participants make their responses simultaneously, but cannot hear the other teams during the response time. After the answers have been presented, the Moderator and her team prepare the responses for all groups to hear.

The online audience is asked to vote on their preferred responses from the teams. The votes are posted at a national social media site. The votes are based upon which responses were the most: seriously considered (including long-term ramifications,) maturity, informed, and genuinely sincere.

From the Viewer's perspective
The screen reads, "*Life*Bowl^sm TV"

Within the screen are two smaller screens, currently set to blank. The participants' restricted images will eventually be displayed within the frames of the screens.

Introduction by the Moderator
"Good evening and welcome to the first *Life*Bowl^sm. I am your Moderator for the Bowl. Tonight we have two groups of four young men, ranging in age between fourteen and eighteen years. There physical locations are kept secret and neither their names, nor any other attributes will be made known to anyone during this program. We also asked them to share their "real" thoughts and feelings on the topics in their responses.

To date, none of the team members have graduated from high school. They agreed to the rules for participating in the **Bowl** and have said so in the presence of one or more parents. The parent or parents of each young man are watching the **Bowl** from an adjoining room at both locations. They have signed waivers and other legal release documents in the presence of retained lawyers. Finally, we wish to thank our sponsors, technical support and others, all of whom have requested to remain anonymous."

Background Program Note:

The two screens open and we see four pairs of hands for each screen. The young men were given two days to prepare for the competition. In preparation for this and two forthcoming sessions, they and their immediate families, were housed in resorts in undisclosed locations. The teams were given three coaches (each), to help them organize and articulate their thoughts, work as a team, and use their "smarts." Every member was continually video taped, so he could see his emotional reactions and listen to his responses.

The teams were also coached in how to support one another, especially given they had never met before their coaching sessions at the resorts. The members of each team were matched for academic aptitudes, critical thinking skills, and general world knowledge. The issue of depth and breadth of vocabularies was left untouched.

The Set-Up

Our view of each participant does not go above the midpoint of his chest. Each sweatshirt has *Life*Bowl^sm stenciled on the front.

Moderator

"Let's begin!"
"Gentlemen, Is everyone ready, please lift your right hand."
All comply.

"Very well, then here is your first question: If a young man "gets" a girl pregnant, what do you think are his responsibilities to the mother and his child?"

What follows are the transcripts, per question, from each team.

Team One
Nothing! We agreed that the girl's parents and the rest of her family should take care of the child. It is their child and not the young man's. He is not required nor expected to remain in her life. How does he know the child is actually his?

Team Two
The members of our tem believe the young man is financially, to the best of his ability, and morally, responsible to support the upbringing of a child he helped bring into the world. The real question is whether he and the girl are mature enough to effectively raise a child, when they may still be "children" themselves?

Moderator
Members of the audience, please reflect and vote on the responses of the team.

"Next question:
What would happen within your respective communities, if private and governmentally supported social services were to disappear? Who would be affected and what do you think should replace those services?"

Transcript of Responses
Team One
A riot would happen, as a lot of people would lose their jobs and the people would not receive money.

Team Two
It would force a lot of people to rethink their futures. Some individuals would undoubtedly try to exploit the situation; but not necessarily to the benefit of the community. We know very little about this historical point, but it sounds like a "carpet bagging" opportunity in the making.

Moderator

"Next Question

How should we close the "gap" or "gaps" between the test results of native born African American boys and White boys in the eighth and then 11th grade levels of school?"

Transcript of responses

Team One

Quit trying to close it for it cannot be done! The gaps are there and won't, excuse us, we won't see a change in our lifetimes. Our parents and communities really don't care about test scores. They are meaningless in our world. It's all a bunch of political, ah, hyper something! We are sorry but in all honesty that is a no brainer question.

Team Two

It is a curious question based upon an even more curious assumption. It presumes there is one, definitive answer to a multi-plex challenge. Our immediate thought is that the families play a key role through continually challenging their children to grow up. They must press on their children to grow up—intellectually, emotionally, and educationally. Specifically, they must study harder than they play and study through out the year and day.

Effective parents know a school day is 24 hours long, seven days a week, fifty-two weeks a year, and for life. It is a habit and nothing less. The purpose of all of this is to make a person strong enough to survive in the world. Otherwise, we insist that school districts and teacher unions have the integrity of purpose and tenacity to get rid of administrators and teachers, who neither want to work with students nor care about them as human beings.

Moderator

"Next Question:

When you look at your neighborhoods and communities in which you live, which organizations genuinely care about the welfare of the children and families living there? How do you know they care?"

<u>Transcripts of Responses</u>

Team One

This isn't a joke. You can tell which organizations care by the quality of cars driven by their staff members—their employees. To put it clearly, how expensive and flashy are the cars? Just drive by and look at the parking lots. What message does that tell you and their "clients?"

Team Two

You walk in and sit down and watch how people, including the youngest and the oldest, are treated by staff members – including the top bosses. Do they walk by people, ignoring their presence, not even saying hello or taking time to acknowledge they are living. Are they "for real people?" Do they want to "CARE" or simply grab and run with the money because it is there? All you have to do is sit, watch, listen, even with your eyes closed.

You can tell who really cares by how they express their interests in the welfare of each person as a human being, regardless of social, ethnic, economic, age or emotional standing. Above all else, and this is critical from our experiences and expectations, those who truly care respect the dignity and humanity of others. That's what we would want to do and would do in their positions, if given the chance and challenge of expectations. We could say more, but that is enough said.

Moderator

"Next Question:

What do people remember about Martin Luther King?"

Team One
Nothing!

Team Two
His "I have a dream" speech. That's all we hear about him and we guess that is all we are suppose to know about him. What else did he do is a mystery to us. In fact, the whole Civil Rights movement is a mystery to us. People seem to assume we should know about that stuff, but our world is in total disconnect from history, even that history.

Moderator
"Next Question:
Who owns you? "

Transcript of Responses
Team One
No one.

Team Two
No one.

Moderator
"Next Question:
From your collective perspectives, what makes a real man in your community and on TV?" "Oops! I am sorry we have run out of time for this session. I apologize!"
The answer for that and other questions will be provided during our next two sessions.

On behalf of the participants, our sponsors, staff and others we thank you for participating. Please remember to post your votes on the responses of the team members.

In addition, we will add two more teams for the two remaining sessions.
End of Session

Please follow-up by reading the additional installments in Book Two, Second session of the competition. In Book Three we include transcripts of conversations with selected team members -- before and after the sessions.

You can also find more thoughts on Soul Rot at:
Wordpress: http://SoulRot.wordpress.com
Web: www.soulrot.info
Twitter.com/soulrotcafe

Chapter Six:
Life's Realities Need You,
Our Perfect Black Man

A Letter to Johnson Taylor Trout

I have known Johnson for about 10 years as he used to hang out with my younger brother. I always thought he was a fun-loving young man. He knew what he wanted to do in life and was willing to sacrifice life's little pleasures in order to achieve his dreams. I was wrong. How sorry I am!

J.T. seemed so careful around people, always apologizing for any slight. He never said anything bad about anyone, even when they deserved it. J.T. was a genuinely nice man. That is the best I can say about my friend.

What did I miss seeing? The question has haunted me for two years, two unhappy and fittingly painful years. And my inescapable personal inquisition continues on and on. Will my life ever find peace again? Will I always see his funny smile in every young black man's face from here to tomorrow? Oh that poor boy! All I want is a little peace and rest, please God please!

The dream is over and it is morning. I felt damp from perspiration as the night's sleepless ordeal gives rise to my mind's feeling the dread and foreboding moments to come. I can only think about what I will have to do later today. It is never pleasant, when I must do my job to the best of my ability. You must be strong, my friend in Japan is always insisting. Be strong, he reminds me, for if you are not who will be for the rest of us?

Funny my friend Joe is saying that in my mind, when I need someone else to be strong for me. How not so funny it is that you are never around when I need your support. Only the wispy memories in my ears from our long walks, along the tapered streets of Gion remain. The wires of progress were strung above us, across the valleys of blocked-shape pavement, so thick that birds needed radar to find their way in broad daylight.

There was peace there and then. Everything made so much sense as well. But then again, everything always makes sense when you're far from home.

I guess I better go back to get to work and quit feeling sorry for myself. How pitiful it would seem if I'd let others know my feelings. But my friend, Johnson, I must let you know, I absolutely have to let you know. I wouldn't be fair to not let you know.

I'm writing to you from my office. I have drawn the curtains closed as the eastern light filters through where it can. But for the blue of the flat screen the room is a somber color, dulled to a dark magistrate gray. I feel cold even though it is summer and the AC is on low. I'm sitting so I must begin this most painful of letters.

Johnson T., I feel uneasy writing to you today for I know my brother would have wanted to talk with you. But he isn't here and I will have to serve as the substitute. Our parents would have loved to talk to you as well. But as you know they passed away five years ago in that awful accident. So I have to do it.

Sad it isn't that such times can't continue forever. I have wished so many moments, every day. I have wished that could happen. What did we do so wrong that we lost you Johnson T.? I just want to know. I feel like crying, you remember how I like to cry and how you and my brother could make me cry so easily.

Wait a minute please okay, okay; I'm okay now. I am trying to make things different for you, but my hands are tied Johnson. I am sorry, it's just I couldn't fight the truth. You couldn't fight to choose and look where that has placed us.

Laugh if you can, I am sure you can see the irony in all of this. Personally, I don't want to see anything, I just want this day to go away forever but not you. I just want the pain to go away that is all I can want now. And you my brother's friend what would you want from me, my brother?

I am thinking of you my brother. I can hear your thoughts. But I can't change history. I can only direct what is to be done.

You want me to save him but I cannot, that's not for you, nor for myself to decide. He's doomed!

I wish we could chat some more, but it is too late. I know where you are right now, my brother's friend. Do you really think I want you to leave; yes others may want you to leave but I don't. This is too permanent, life should be permanent don't you think? Will you let me sleep tonight? It is late in the afternoon and I must finish this letter and make the final decision so many are waiting for me to make.

I wish you were here with me. No, I am glad you are not here. Now I understand.

The door opens and all rise as the judge looks down at Johnson Taylor Trout. He has just finished a letter to himself foretelling a terminal event of his life. He looks at the judge who seems both so distant and so friendly, while so deadly serious. She should be serious as it is the beginning of the end of days, a judgment day, for Johnson Taylor Trout.

Mr. Johnson Taylor Trout, you are hereby condemned to death!

The teacher put down the paper, which had been written by one of her 9th grade students. She looked up the faces of twenty-five young men and women. No one was crying and no one laughed. She asked how many knew young men like Johnson Taylor Trout?

All raised their hands.

Chapter Seven: Next?
That is where we go from here!
Maybe!

* Next Happened! Where were you?

If we look back approximately 20 to 25 years ago, we would find there was an enormous opportunity for Black communities to embrace computer technologies. That did not happen!

Obviously, there were individuals, who did engage the future. Unfortunately, there was still an insurmountable wall of unwillingness to look at technology as an opportunity. Specifically, computers were invisible. Ironically, the "invisible" could not see the invisible.

It was not about money as much about a lack of vision, ambition, inspiration, perspiration and curiosity. Those communities still pay a heavy price for their intellectual negligence and patented indifference to the future.   **Why?**

I believe that the general and historical attitudes of many Black Americans leans towards anti-technology[6]. Or at least it has been up to recent years and a lot of that has to do with cultural taboos. Older Black Americans would look at such things and say that's not something "we do!"[7]

---

[6] Many Black Americans have made huge contributions in the world of science, technology, space, weather, sound, computers, software, food science, chemistry, math, history, anthropology, physics, you name it. It is just, well, most Black-African-Americans don't know those facts.   Too many started listening to the "song" about not trying to learn hard things in school.

[7] Obviously, Black Americans are not alone in holding that belief.

It is also a perennial issue: "that's something those people do, those people being white Americans." This is a pervasive attitude among many Black Americans. It represents intellectual stagnation or a "self-dumbing-down" effect. Let's go a little further.

Is it hard to understand why so many people tag studying and learning, as something we should not do as a people? Whatever the reason it seems people are sworn, culturally, to turn a blind eye to the necessities behind learning. For instance, generation after generation adhere to doing the minimal levels of work in school to just get by. It's a form of getting over on the system.

About Progress

So we have the schools: we have some good teachers and we have some inadequate, down right bad teachers. Of course, we have libraries and now the Internet. What else do we need to progress or regress?

Take a look at the prisons. There is a tolerance for people going to jail. I repeat, there is a tolerance for people going to jail! Young men are expected to pass a ritual, the right of a modern middle passage, an escape tunnel from daily life. Many others are sanctioned by: their families, their neighborhoods, and their communities, to discover a life in prison.

What would happen if their families, neighborhoods and communities, sanctioned their embracing the future through earning an education?

A prison is a place where young men are squeezed into cells for actions that were totally unnecessary, and thus avoidable. But as a culture, those activities mimic self-destructive behavior. Like lemmings running, no racing to the cliff, at the edge of the Abyss they stop, but are pushed off by the weight of the rush behind them.

Those at the back of the crowd hear a faint yell of: **"Stop My People!"** But when you are in the back of the crowd, stop means – **"What did they say?" "I don't know, but let's keep moving that away, something must be going on up there and we don't want to miss the action."**

Also, think of the squirrel that makes it halfway across the street. A car quickly converges on him and suddenly he reverses direction! **Road kill!** Yes, but was it an accident?

If there is a Plan to this inherit madness, then I believe some self-appointed members, in a few Black communities, have written the Plan themselves. Of course, some might insist it must be God's Plan. Please! Don't fake a divine alliance. None of us are God!

It isn't God's Plan. Keep God out of it unless you truly believe some Black and some White people are God. If so, I suggest you better have a long conversation, through prayer, with God. God might want to educate you on THE TRUTH! We don't tell God who is or should be in The Plan, least of all ourselves.

The Briefing

Dr. Jonathan Theodore Kobayashi
March, 2011
Another King's Speech and Million's of Opportunities Lost

I recently listened to someone reciting Martin Luther King's 1963, "I have a dream" speech. I'm old enough to have heard the original given on that particular and curious day.

Back then everyone, who cared about the future, were moved by what they heard. The words provided only a signal for Hope, where many had never known the sound of the word in their lives. Yet, it was only one speech among dozens upon dozens, he made during his brief life time. His writings and letters far outnumbered the words counted in the 1963 speech. In my opinion, many of his writings have had far greater importance than that one speech.

But, who has read his other writings? It is a pitiful shame to be known for just one speech. Even one as significant as "I Have A Dream,"

If you look for contemporary accounts of the speech, within a week of his giving it in 1963, you'll see very little written about it. In my opinion, it gained viral brand quality, only after his death in 1968. Let me ask you: <u>who today really listens and takes to heart</u> what he said that day? Has the context of our present lives made it difficult to understand, why its importance was validated by one momentous day in history?

Also, after reflecting, who thinks about what he didn't include in his speech? This last point is critical for understanding the prognosis for the Perfect Black Man's future in our evolving American society and the World.

Please consider why King chose to put the onus of responsibility, for the welfare of the future of Black men and women, on the shoulders of people, who are not Black by birth? It was a political sermon. The politics were Black, cultural and over the power of leadership and direction of a movement.

He had the ears of the world listening to him. Yet, I believe he under utilized the best moment in his life. He could have forever accelerated the advancement of an extraordinary future for all Black Americans, American women, immigrants and all other people living in America.

What he did say helped promote Hope. Unfortunately, it did not create a map to grow a cultural discipline. It did not activate what Hope is designed to support and sustain.

In my opinion, Hope needed, then and now, millions of roadmaps to help chart millions of financially, politically and socially productive lives waiting to start.

Besides hearing that short, stirring speech by Dr. King, the crowds should have been treated to other speeches on why independence in living had to become a keystone for their futures. The throngs of listeners, on the ground in Washington and around America, could have heard why and how to create viable, economic futures for their families and communities. They needed to hear "Yes, you can make it so! Yes, we can make it so!"

Other speakers were needed to inspire faith among aspiring youth, towards goals reaching beyond their parents' wildest dreams. Millions needed to see living people, who did not fear leading the future of the world. Women, men and children would have heard words about building mountains, exploring the heavens and the seas. They would have been incited to engage learning to become masters of our universe of knowledge. In that sphere, their parents would have been rewarded, through watching their children, overcome the ravages of centuries of legalized ignorance.

More importantly, we needed to hear words about overcoming our fears of ourselves, and our socially repressive taboos.

Finally, and most importantly, we needed to hear how we had to face and overcome our fears about valuing, developing and applying --- the intelligence given, equally, to all people on the earth by God.

I truly wish we had heard those speeches, on that day, from the steps of the Lincoln Memorial. It was a perfect day for the world to listen to history and to learn why and how to create a more perfect future.

We have to accept that our futures are in our minds, our hands and in how we apply our souls. It has been said, that minds can be wasted. Yes, they can be and are diluted every day. The same can be said as well for souls. They too can rot away, out of disuse, abuse and neglect.

We have already allowed too many millions to escape the future, by sweeping themselves under the mats of co-dependent bureaucracies, and suffer the quiet humiliation of fearing themselves. Yes, we let them waste away. We let them grow up to rot.

The next time you see a baby in the arms of its mother, who is herself still a child; will you see a future entrepreneur in technology, or an outstanding candidate, waiting to become another Perfect Black Man?
Thank you, Dr. Jonathan Theodore Kobayashi

A Commentary
By Michael Mason Norman, ED.D.
March, 2011

Few dreams in our lives are ever awarded. For those realized, we pay a princely tribute as rent to live an existence favored by reality and fate.

In actuality, we deserve nothing in our lives, except our heart beats and the breadths of air we consume. If we yearn for Hope to deliver us from evil, we must earn Hope. No matter how treacherous the path we must follow, Hope begets Hope. It does so only for those undaunted by the unknowns of the future and the memories, which shadow our pasts!

Are we really "free at last?" Those words "free at last" seem ancient to my ears. We are free from a legacy of history, if we want to be. Yet that freedom is dependent upon how free you feel comfortable in your skin. Please look around you, can you truly and honestly say you're free to be yourself? Do you know who you are? Be honest!

I don't want to hear any amen's or right on's. Please don't say "amen brother," unless you mean it from the depths of your hearts. My patience is at an end with people, who say something they don't really mean.

The world is full of self-serving, purveyors of passive-aggressiveness. Where words are empty and finding authentic personalities come at a premium. Looking over my shoulders, I see into the shadows where creepy creatures go lurking. They are called hubris, disciples of Napoleonic superiority, mendacity and xenophobia. These human vermin wait to devour unguarded Hope, wherever it is found.

Let me shift

Do you believe in HOPE? I do believe in Hope, but my Hope is going to make you very uncomfortable. You will surprise me if you are not dutifully angry after reading the following pages. Take a moment and look into a mirror with your anger. Who do you see?

Hope, when validated through the discipline of introspection, requires an unmitigated understanding of human nature. Set below is a direct human application of HOPE. You won't find it in a smartphone APP Store. At least not yet.

Absent stupidity or greed, shackling a person to a self-limiting ideology, robs him of freedom of thought and movement. When Black America's future was shackled to a so-called "debt owed to it," the forward progress of the traditional Civil Right's movements -- stopped, almost cold. (my opinion)

People halted closely held efforts to expand their worlds and eventually sought shelter inside Boxes. Consequently, Black Americans developed increasingly impoverished self-esteems, and impoverishing imaginations. Instead of creating independent businesses, we learned to dine on entitlements; which by the way, replaced our hard earned freedom from dependency and tilted "Places." We became free to no longer think for ourselves and know ourselves.

Predictably, things became very interesting. You know, we are a very predictable people!

Minds began closing!

Throughout the days of the Civil Rights movements, we did not invest inheritable self-discipline, of "scaled-up" responsibilities, into 35 million diversified life portfolios. Again, we expected, i.e., shackled ourselves, into believing that governments would take care of us, by simply protecting us from the pasts. In so doing we abandoned our increasingly progressive roots and roles. We ignored rules of discipline to grow, as taught by success in overcoming failure.

The roles waited for us--patiently. Our roots began to rot. The future was there for us to create it. Instead, we handed over those roles and responsibilities to others. They became our "saviors," so to speak. We learned to fear our futures, by learning to fear and mistrust ourselves.

It is my personal belief, that Black America has let ignorance of economics and our own human fears, place us in sets of shifting, deeply cut and out-dated cultural ruts. Inside the walls of the ruts, we managed to master: neglecting, destroying and soundly disowning the future, at both personal and community levels. Ultimately, we bankrupted tomorrow and let our dreams succumb to identity-foreclosure.

Where Did We Go From There?
Here Happened Next!

Black America voluntarily disenfranchised itself from: progress; legitimate business opportunities; development of technological wonders; ambition; free will; responsible parenthood; intellectual growth; scientific pursuits; creativity; craftsmanship; exploration; material wealth for generations to come; world changing teaching, and so one.

To put it simply, we placed the onus of responsibility over our futures into the mindsets of both good and bad people. Some of them were and are not Black by birth and some were and are Black by birth.

What I want to make perfectly clear, to all reading this material: the prospects for our futures (Black or native born African Americans,) are not dependent upon what others do for us, nor to us.

Our futures are totally dependent upon what we do for and to ourselves.
But some will say, "They tell us we are victims, so we must be! Right?"

A majority of the world's people are victims. Are we any different, are we somehow "exceptionalized" as victims? How convenient.

Victims?

The Perfect Black Man fits this socially-regressive landscape
very well. The PETS even better.

He doesn't even have to work at it.
Are we today greater, more worthy of the title, "victims," than
those in the Sudan, Darfur in particular?

Who should now feel guilt and shame?

What kinds of shoes are you wearing? What did you eat for
lunch, dinner and breakfast and where did you sleep and what
kind of water do you have to drink? Oh, you don't drink water,
just sodas! How thoughtless of me.

What did you do to the Sudanese,
the Res. tribes, families in barrios?
And, please don't forget those kids, whose families were pushed
out of their homes through real foreclosures.

Let me not forget the dude who stole all of his Grandmother's
money she was saving for her old age. Why? He needed some
wheels! All of a sudden the "victim" creates a real victim.
Except he has no guilt and shame.

What does guilt and shame do to you?

Go to Haiti, its close, if you need a qualified reality check on guilt
and shame. Again, if you need something closer, I think we can
find some places in rural America: like do or probably die at
ram-shackled farms. You ever visited a remnant of a slave's
plot? I think there are some still about the land. For the moment
I am forgetting their present day name. It makes a sweet sound.
These are not atypical places waiting to be officially declared as
victim-hoods. While you look around those spots of indignities,
look for social service agencies, competing with one another to
help the "victims," help themselves.

What do they have over the PBM's street?

**"They tell us we are stupid, lazy and unimportant in the big scheme of things,
so we are! Right?"**

........Apply this thought........

Upon M.L. King, Jr.'s death, PBM's burned down some of our communities, in order to make us free from something. So what is left?

We, also shoot up some of our communities, with drugs and guns.

Let's Look At What Is Really Going On: Again, it is my opinion.

Fear Mongering Shops and Catatonics

Fear mongering shops are non-fact based, propaganda front-loaded stores for hysterics. Yes, they are stores. In fact, I don't think we can honestly categorize them as conspiracies at all. In America the stores serve as places for a buying public needing supplies to emotionally retreat to an America, which never existed.

In short, there are people who want to regress to a land of myth, beyond the reach of historic reality and the legends and values, which formed this country. Fear mongering shops cater to their needs, wants and desires. Do not fear these stores, unless you fear Hope.

Here is an Idea worth thinking about.

My Idea is to bankrupt the fear mongers, using one of their classic weapons of mass societal destruction.

I believe fear mongers need enemies; all inherently imagined, and reconstructed for maximum local impact! Their stores sell all the material and media goods to "True Believers," who need enemies to energize and justify their sensitivities of being unjustly made victims of history. Their leaders believe they have the moral high ground, when the land is flat and they live in life's emotional gutters, full of hate and distorted thinking.

We need to remember that the so-called "Moral Majority" was neither a majority in America and through its tactics, left many wondering about their claim in being pillars of high "moral" values. Their moralizing was often not supported by their actions. We will again see a variant of this group starting a year from now, if not already.

Fear mongers and their clients believe in working themselves into frenzies about things they truly don't nor want to understand. These are people not known for having critical thinking skills. I believe many have lived decades without a word of curiosity about the world passing their lips.

Right now they need a figurative debt for a rallying point; let's presume it is owed by America to Black America. They also need a poster boy: My nomination for that role is the Perfect Black Man.

Next Happens! Fear Mongers, Now Hear This

As in the past Black America WILL defend what it means to be an American. We will help overcome the next tempest within the shores and borders of its 50 states, territories and other lands.   Keeping America Free From Purveyors of Fear

Whatever comes our way as a nation, we will overcome it! As throughout America's history, our skills, intelligence, perseverance, and self-respect will prevail over all adversities: both human and events driven by nature.

More importantly, Black Americans know what it means to be treated worse than animals. Native Americans know this and continue experiencing this point everyday. Of course, they are not the only ones in America, who have experienced being treated as objects of exploitation.

Look at most descendants of immigrants in America: Viet Namese, Hmong, Thais, North Africans, Indians from India, Irish, serfs, Jews, Haitians, Koreans, Serbs, Pakistanis, Afghans, native Alaskans, Christians, Baptists, Catholics, Iranians, Iraqis, Mennonites, Amish, Croats, Pilgrims, former residents from Caribbean islands, Russians, Chinese, Japanese, Poles, Hispanics, Latinos, to just name a few. The list is long. It covers the world.

Our collective futures unite us against the destabilizing control of organized ignorance and fear, when they are aligned with emotional imbalance. Especially when those "cults of regression" are enhanced by disruptive, abusive rerouting of human thinking and unprotected memories.

We must counter 1930's and 40's styles propaganda techniques, with impenetrable, and untouchable facts and HOPE for many better tomorrows.

It is about overcoming those who want to overcome us. And we have been there and I promise you that is not going to happen again.

FearBots
Let me introduce the infamous four headless, remote controlled FearBots. They are charged to override and then reroute the hyper-sensitized minds of the historically challenged, fact-phobic, emotionally insecure and (dis)-stablized by life's events.

They live in a mentally myopic **screen-world**. Such a world shelters a tube full of: simple stick images, simple stories, simple concepts and populated for and with simple people, with simple needs and ideas.

It is a place where by making things simple, life is made simpler, but not better.

Here we find a play land for adults, who need political and economic reality daycare.

The four headless Fearbots

They ride electronic circuits and are remotely controlled from somewhere. The Fearbots are never held accountable for their actions or words. They own those who buy their influence. Here they are, in order of impact:

- Ignorance and fear about the world and America's place within it. Fear of religions other than their own interpretation's of their own religion, lives inside this Fearbot;

-

- Fears of the unknown and of things, which require more than a fourth grade education. For example, current events. At this point life must be explained to them using made-for-children tales and illustrated through graphically non-challenging drawings;

-

- Abandonment, resignation and divorce from progressive, capitalistic and intellectually engaged, highly accountable management practices and socially responsible American values. This FearBot fears documented facts.

-

- Xenophobia, fear of youth, fear of technology, fear of what the elderly represent, and catatonic reactions to economically/socially/educationally mixed communities.

You may know more, but those will suffice for this discussion.

OK, HERE WE GO!
This is my take on J.T. Kobayashi's briefing.

Black Americans are Americans and, we are owed NOTHING by The United States of America!

Except: equal access to and use of those opportunities, which bind the country together through its laws, protections, rights, values, rules of fair play, economic imperatives and faith and realization of justice and freedom for all, and not just for a self-selected few.

Black Americans:
Less we forget: We are Americans and we are citizens and like all American citizens, we are nothing less in the eyes of the law.

America and Democracy are The Rule of Law and cannot disappear and will not change as long as America is America.

In addition to what I stated above, we, you and me are not owed debts made through slavery, over a hundred years ago. Instead, we need to exploit the use of our brains to create our own personal wealth.   This includes challenging governments to meet contractual and statutory agreements. For example, a landmark case set by Black farmers in the South. A government cannot pay some, while ignoring to pay comparable recipients.

That is a little twist on the myths some of us hold about ourselves. As we can achieve whatever goals we set, through persistent pursuits of creative and productive market driven enterprises.   We have rights under the laws of the lands. We must protect them by using the law and to protect the laws as well. Otherwise, we may silently strike a deal to negate our claims as Americans and citizens.

Hang in there, we are heading to the closing
There is another little twist to this story, I must tell you and I hope you sit back and absorb the words, without reacting out of self-pity and self-defensiveness.

Let's Twist Irony Upon Itself

Are PBM's heroes? Or, are they scripted to obey the fatalistic expectations of social myths?

A set of beliefs, govern Perfect Black Men and FearBot-owned True Believers.

There is a little secret I will share with you:

FearBots and PBM's share common, social inferiority complexes.

Consider the following non-exhaustive list:

Just Checking and Messing **With Your Mind**

A. Whites and others must change from ways of bigotry, before Black men and women can progress and feel free. **Is that true or false?**

B. Whites must end racism towards Blacks, especially in the treatment of the manhood of Black men. **T or F**

C. Equality must be established in order to give Hope to Black men. **True or False**

D. Whites must feel continually guilty for slavery. **T or F**

E. Black men are kept inferior by poverty and racism. **T or F**

F. Black men have little self-esteem because they are not suppose to have it, nor can they achieve self-esteem through means of their own. **False   or   True**

G. All Black men must gain equality, together, or none will have any sense of freedom and equality. (It is assumed that all Whites have equality.) **True or False**

H. Anyone who is not a PBM is a sell-out and is not truly Black and should not be listened to, nor inspire respect. **True or False**

I. The PBM needs racists to continue feeling oppressed and thus not have to achieve anything socially productive during his life. This includes not becoming a devoted and supportive father to his children. **True or False**

J. PBM's do not own their lives and do not have to learn how to live in the world as masters of their own fates. **True or False**

K. All White people are smart and because they are smart, Black men cannot be smart; so they don't need to learn anything because to do so means they must "act White." To "act White" means you are no longer Black and thus not real. To not be real means you make yourself an outsider and outsiders have no place among PBM's. **Therefore,** to be a successful PBM you must not be smart, like Whites and not associate with Blacks, who are smart and thus are "acting White." **True or False**

L. The invisible Black community, where "invisible men" are found, does not trust "acting White" Black men. They prefer to keep PBM's within the community, where they look inward and accept their fate, because that makes the community feel better and safer. Therefore, PBM's enjoy and need to remain PBM's for the good of their communities and security of a collective identity. **True or False**

M. All White people are successful and have extremely high IQ's and self-esteems. **True or False**

O. All Black people are financially poor and destitute. **True or False.**

P. All White people are wealthy billionaires?
True or False

The Twists

In the minds of "invisible men," responses to the above questions must come from Whites, who accept their responsibilities as enablers. With this admission, White's are required to undertake caring for Black men, women and children through perpetuity. Such is the price of the sins attributed to the ancestors of a few Whites, companies, religions and governments.

This includes: police, politicians, social service groups, some teachers, some political activists; whose futures are dependent upon PBM's remaining ineffective as individuals. On the surface, it appears that all of these groups are dominated by Whites; but look very closely as some are staffed and led by Black men and women.

For some reason it is believed Whites are the only racists in the world and by definition Blacks cannot be racist because they are Black and discriminated by all Whites. Oops, Blacks also discriminate against other blacks, over things like skin tone, too black or too tan ("yellow".) There is more, but that is another long list, which is too long to include in a small book.

It is said, Blacks cannot discriminate against any other minority group member out of professional courtesy. Uh, that cannot be true. If you said yes, we need to send you through a little therapy. Of course, all other minorities in the world, never discriminate against one of their "own kind." Never? Members of majority groups, don't discriminate against members of their groups. Nope! Religions don't discriminate against members of their groups, either. Members of families don't discriminate against members of their own families. A father would never steal from his family!

Back to our earlier topic: Two Point Reversal Twist

Inside select groups, no one says Whites should stop their careers as enablers. That is a no-win situation for all, especially the enabled PBM's.

Another twist involves presenting behavioral patterns fitting stereotypical images of Black men. For example, those who need the PBM, find themselves reinforcing the images. For example, certain news (crime stories) and sports media, clothing advertising groups, and fear mongers, come to mind among many venues of electronically based social influence. PBM's sell!

Finally, when we are confronted with the question: "Where do we go from here?" we must remember that *here* is found in many places. All of which are formed from dissimilar assumptions, which lead to a multitude of possible directions. Then perspectives, drawn to analyze this recurring human spectacle, will outnumber the count of assumptions. From there the conclusions will continue growing and evolving, until the question is no longer asked for there was never a definitive answer to be found.

Remember my friends,

Find racism and bigotry and you find ignorance and fear.

Find ignorance and fear and you find people. Find people, well you find people, but not necessarily racism, unless you need to find it, and then your eyes will discover whatever you want to see.

Find the non-Perfect Black Man and you find the beginning of the end of one form of Soul Rot.

———

Yes, there are many variations on the theme of---

Soul Rot.

Closure

A note from the author:

I truly appreciate your reading the material in Book One on Soul Rot. Soul Rot is a three dimensional concept and requires viewing from several perspectives. I addition, I know the stories probably felt disjointed and not in sequence. The structure of the book represents the life of a Perfect Black Man, as I have envisioned and interpreted.

His world is not nice and linear like those of normal people. When we add the influences of our increasingly electronic social media age, he cannot escape and hide in a quiet space. He can never be himself.

The pace of life is genuinely increasing for him and for the rest of us as well. Consequently, his ability to progress out of the box, by escaping the reaches of its hidden anarchies, becomes ever more problematic and predictably unsuccessful.

When we look at the multitude of research studies, Foundation and governmental based support systems; we wonder what would happen to our PBM, if all that money were spent, directly, on his education? What would become of him? How much of the money supports a set of industries, rather than actually supporting his escape from the Box?

But then again, maybe the industries represent a different set of boxes for him to jump into. Is he expected to escape from all of the boxes? At least you can escape colleges and universities (just in theory.)

The two remaining books on Soul Rot: Escaping the Box, will merge many additional topics, which serve as signposts and landmarks in the world of The Perfect Black Man.

Between now and their release, I hope you have time to think about what should become of The Perfect Black Man and his counter culture replacement—The Imperfect Black Man? If you would like to add any thoughts about **their** futures, please comment at one of the social media sites for Soul Rot.

Again, thank you for participating in the world of The Perfect Black Man and Soul Rot.
Michael Mason Norman, ED.D.
March, 2011

YouTube Channel: SoulRotCodes Opening in late March, 2011
Wordpress: http://SoulRot.wordpress.com
Web: www.soulrot.info
Twitter.com/soulrotcafe   email: soulrotcafe@soulrot.info

Many thanks to friends around the
world, who have put up with my
questions, more honestly (inquisitions),
over the years.
We will forget the other weird stuff.

This book is dedicated to the memory
of the following very important people
in my life:

Thomas Roy Norman, Saphronia
Norman Renfro
Lutischie and Booker Mason
Mr. and Mrs. Alonzo Redman, Sr.
Mrs. Josie Logan, The Kenneth Logan
family, Dr. William Ross, Mr. and Mrs.
Marshall Penn, Col. Spurgeon Moore
and family, Dr. Joe Woods
Mr. Lucius Jones
Phil Pennington, Andrew Roberts
The Hardimans, Mr. and Mrs. I. J
Collier, Dr. Oscar Anderson Fuller,
Dr. Lorenzo Greene and family,
The Norman's, The West's
The Robinson's, Bo Hannon
Rev. Edgar L. Reid and family
The Pullum family, The Fulbright's
The Bell's, The Hoard's, The White's

Michael Mason Norman, ED.D.
A Master Teacher For People Who
Love Learning
An Insatiable Learner For Students
An Incomparable Listener For People Who
Think For A Living

The author is an educator, mentor, and worksite development consultant. He specializes in creating adaptive work settings for progressive, client-centered, organizations. He coaches employees and managers on creating new, productive work activities. Mike also, conducts strategic planning sessions for non-profit and governmental organizations. Finally, he conducts web-based career advisory sessions, with professionals in many fields. His consulting experiences have spanned over 24 years

Dr. Norman has worked in a number of fields, including: mental health, K-12 special education, higher education administration, sales training, non-profit-research/administration/fundraising, undergraduate and graduate teaching in business management and leadership.

Originally from Jefferson City, Missouri, he has lived in Seattle, Washington and Wisconsin. Currently, he is a resident of Minnesota.   Mike is also a double graduate from the University of Missouri--Columbia.

Reading, photography, fly fishing, pheasant hunting, and video work are his passions. Yes, he is investing more time in writing; while world travel is always trying to kidnap him from his work.

Mike truly enjoys talking with old friends, making new friends, and continually learning from new and former students.